PORTLAND'S
100 BEST PLACES
TO STUFF YOUR FACES

SECOND EDITION

A lovingly-curated insider's guide to
the most delicious, delightful and
unique dining experiences
in Portland, Oregon.

Written by JEN STEVENSON

Second Edition

ISBN 978-0-9833958-2-9

Copyright © 2013

Wordcake Communications

PO Box 4081

Portland, OR 97208

www.underthetablewithjen.com

Written,

designed & printed

exclusively in Portland, OR.

All restaurants are locally owned.

Although I went to great pains to ensure that all the information in this book
was 100 percent accurate and fresh as a just-picked heirloom tomato as of the
press date, things can change instantly in the food world. Restaurants shutter
or relocate unexpectedly, chefs and owners part ways or move to Martinique,
favorite dishes and happy hours appear and disappear, hours lengthen with
the summer sun and shrivel in the dark days of winter. So before you embark
on an eating adventure, it never hurts to double check the facts.

BEST PLACES TO STUFF YOUR FACES TEAM

Writer, Researcher, Chief Face Stuffer .... *Jen Stevenson*

Designer, Creative Director, Ruthlessly Efficient Dane .... *Mette Hornung Rankin*

Copy Editor, Production Manager, Eagle Eye .... *Shellie Anderson*

FOR THE AMAZING M'S IN MY LIFE
Thank goodness for you all, and for your appetites.

TABLE OF CONTENTS

♦

TABLE SCRAPS

INTRODUCTION

Since I published the first edition of this guide, Portland's dining scene has continued to rise faster than a Red Fife boule made with wild beard yeast, and as always, my trusty fork and I feel very grateful to be in the middle of the feeding frenzy.

Extraordinary eating opportunities continue to abound in the City That Never Stops Eating, and it was incredibly difficult to narrow them down to a hundred. The locally-owned destinations in this book are my personal favorites, chosen for their deliciousness, personality, and the unique Portland experience they offer. Visiting them, I hope you get a sense of the irrepressible spirit and creativity of Portland's intrepid chefs, bakers, chocolatiers, cheesemongers, pizzaiolos, farmers, restaurateurs, and cartrepreneurs. I hope you *don't* get indigestion and a muffin top, but if so, welcome to my world.

As you eat your way through this book, use the handy *Eat Sheet* to check off each spot (see the back cover flap for details). But don't stop at 100! Portland is overflowing with more good food than you can shake a scale at, and for extra credit, you can investigate the hundreds of local eateries catalogued on my website *underthetablewithjen.com*.

Now, off you go on your gastro-walkabout. May you take only dignified bites and leave only crumbs.

Jen

A GUIDE TO THE GUIDE

PRICE

Average cost per diner for a starter and main. If, like me, you tend to accidentally also order a house cocktail, bottle of sparkling rosé, three desserts and a tumbler of nice bourbon, you'll probably overstep these parameters. For shame, piglet!

$...*$10 or less* / **$$**...*$11-$20* / **$$$**...*$21-$40*
$$$$...*More than $40, less than a La Cornue Grand Palais*

HOURS

Current as of the day this book went to press, but they could change at the drop of a piece of buttered toast. Calling before you go is always a good idea.

PARKING

Generally easy to find in most Portland neighborhoods, and comes in two varieties: Metered (coins and credit cards only), and Free (my favorite price). If taking public transportation, easily plan your route at *trimet.org*.

RESERVATIONS

Make them if possible, and remember that waits can be daunting at popular no-reservations establishments during peak face-stuffing hours, particularly for brunch. From one line-phobe to another: go early or go patient.

MUST EATS

Five dishes that captured my stomach's heart. However, many Portland chefs change their seasonal, market-driven menus as often as you change your underwear (I hope), so some might be but a delicious memory when you go. Don't fret, be adventurous!

SIDE DISH

A juicy bonus morsel.

BRIBERY-FREE GUARANTEE

Steering you towards your ideal meal is my number one goal, and all 100 places in this book are my personal favorites and experiences I want to share with you. Rest assured that none of the recommendations were bought, I paid for all of the meals I ate in the pursuit of formulating this book myself, which is why my current retirement plan is to die young, preferably with a glass of champagne and a bar of dark chocolate in hand.

ACCANTO

ITALIAN *in* SUNNYSIDE

Accanto means "near" or "alongside" in Italian, and despite the fact that my house is nearly alongside this cute corner cafe, I don't get to go as often as I'd like, because my job isn't the kind of job that lets you settle down with just one restaurant. But sure, I won't deny that I think about committing to Accanto. After all, it has everything you want in a steady—upbeat energy, good looks, solid kitchen skills and the ability to mix a mean cocktail, plus it cooks brunch every weekend. On Saturday *and* Sunday. It's a tempting package.

Walking in, the always-congenial bartender gives you a smile like he couldn't wait to see you again, even if he's never seen you. Take a seat at the bar, or opt for a table for two in the window, or if the weather is nice, a sidewalk table that gives you a front row view of drivers trying to parallel park without thumping the bumpers of everyone watching them. Up on the wall, a small chalkboard lists the day's specials, and check those first for seasonal gems that often end up being your favorite part of the meal, other than the smoked trout mousse-filled olive oil beignets, pillowy potato gnocchi with rich lamb bolognese, grated Pecorino and fresh mint, juicy roast chicken, squares of homemade peach tart á la mode, and golden ricotta doughnuts with lemon curd for dipping.

Not just a pretty dinner face, your new beau serves brunch faithfully every weekend morning, and you'll likely want to go both days—because who needs to play the brunch field when there are buckwheat crepes drenched in rhubarb compote, Dutch bambinos piled with stone fruit, and cod brandade and piperade Benedicts with saffron hollandaise to be loved? Which go beautifully with the crispy prosciutto-garnished Belmont Bloody, grapefruit mimosa, and Old Overholt and Cointreau-spiked Accanto Coffee. Yes, if only I was a one-restaurant kind of girl. If only!

MUST EATS

Dutch bambino, ricotta doughnuts with lemon curd, olive oil beignets with smoked trout mousse, sage pesto gnocchi, roast chicken

SIDE DISH

With its sumptuous multi-course tasting menu and wine list, Accanto's schmancy neighboring sister restaurant Genoa is just the place for a deluxe birthday, anniversary, retirement, or, provided *you* aren't a commitmentphobe, proposal dinner.

DETAILS	HOURS
• Reservations accepted via phone or *opentable.com*	WED-FRI 11am-3pm
	SUN-THU...... 5:30-11pm
• Street parking is free and easy to find	FRI-SAT 5:30pm-12am
	Brunch
	SAT-SUN 10am-2pm

. . . .

2838 SE BELMONT STREET

503.235.4900 • *accantopdx.com*

. . . .

**$$$**$ *Credit Cards Accepted*

ALMA CHOCOLATE

CHOCOLATE *in* KERNS

The devil is in the 23-carat details at this charming chocolate boutique, a darkly delicious world of devils, saints, and hearts—both anatomically correct and otherwise—molded from 73% single-origin Venezuelan chocolate and hand-gilded with edible 23-carat gold leaf. Needless to say, these choco-icons pack a serious punch come Valentine's Day, but since I believe every day should be V-Day, I see no reason why you shouldn't gently place an Alma icon upon your lover's silk pillow every night.

If pillow truffles are more your style, Alma stocks a selection of blissful bite-sized truffles and bon bons, as well as buttery whiskey caramels, pistachio toffee, marcona almond-studded triple chocolate brownies, salted brown butter wafers, and for those hot summer nights, decadent seasonal choco-pops that are essentially frozen truffles on a stick.

Lovely chocolatier/owner Sarah Hart, who named her exquisite little Northeast Portland shop after her Grandmother Alma, also bakes some of the most sinfully rich chocolate layer cake to ever pass your cacao-loving lips, so leave some of that on your lover's pillow too—nobody's ever been kicked out of bed for eating Alma chocolate cake. I think.

MUST-EATS

Thai peanut butter cup, salty nutty toffee, chocolate frogs, Mom's chocolate cake, dark chocolate peanut butter choco-pop

SIDE DISH

Sarah makes luscious seasonal ice creams for sale in the store and as part of her annual summer CSI (Community Supported Ice Cream) program. The limited memberships sell out in a heartbeat, so keep an eye out for sign-ups and pounce.

DETAILS

• Street parking is free and generally easy to find

HOURS

MON-THUR ... 11am-6pm
FRI-SAT 11am-7pm
SUN.............. 12-5pm

140 NE 28TH AVENUE
503.517.0262 • almachocolate.com

$$$$ *Credit Cards Accepted*

ANDINA

PERUVIAN *in the* PEARL DISTRICT

Oh, the Andina mojito. It's as bewitching as your wicked ex's (admittedly irresistible) blue eyes, except that, unlike your bad romance, this refreshing cocktail is a relationship worth envying—the elusive perfect marriage of lime juice, mint, simple syrup and Appleton white rum over ice, garnished with a stick of sugarcane so crisp its crunch rivals a Sabrett.

And since it's inevitable that when you give a girl a mojito, she'll want some gorgeous Peruvian fare to go with it, it's fortunate that Andina has a tapas selection beyond compare—jewel-like ruby red piquillo peppers stuffed with quinoa and serrano ham, avocado halves overflowing with crab salad and prawns, smoky grilled asparagus, and tiny tender bay scallops baked beneath Parmesan and doused with lime butter, all brought to the table as they are prepared.

The exotic menu is matched by Andina's sophisticatedly-rustic dining room—the vivid colors, gentle archways, gleaming hardwood floors, exposed beams and snaking ductwork meld to create a festive elegance that's always congenial, while staying in step with the posh sensibilities of the surrounding neighborhood. Service is warm and gracious, and if you're lucky, owner "Mama Doris" will stop by your table for a chat as she strolls through the restaurant.

When the last plate has been licked clean and whisked away, you may be tempted to jump up and race to the airport to catch a plane to Lima, but don't leave without having dessert. The crisp quinoa-studded cannoli with passion fruit mousse and mango-lemongrass sorbet is yet another enviable edible romance, and the crème brulée trio would bring a smile even to your moody ex's (admittedly luscious) lips.

MUST EATS

Crab-stuffed avocado, grilled asparagus, spicy tuna causa, green mango and prawn cebiche, quinoa passion fruit cannoli

SIDE DISH

During happy hour, you can kick off your work heels under the table in Mestizo, Andina's adjoining bar, and enjoy discounted drinks, oysters, and anticuchos—skewers of grilled chicken, octopus, and beef heart. Mestizo also hosts live musicians every night of the week; check the website for the current schedule.

DETAILS

- Reservations accepted via phone or *opentable.com*
- Street parking is metered and can be difficult to find

HOURS

DAILY 11:30am-2:30pm
SUN-THU 4-11pm
FRI-SAT 4pm-12am
Happy Hour
DAILY 4-6pm

. . . .

1314 NW GLISAN STREET

503.228.9535 • *andinarestaurant.com*

. . . .

**$$$**$ *Credit Cards Accepted*

APIZZA SCHOLLS

PIZZA *in* SUNNYSIDE

My Apizza Scholls philosophy is very simple. Go for the Apizza Amore, stay for the Apizza Amore. It's the pie I think about for days after our encounter, pining for its swirls of rich housemade tomato sauce, fresh whole milk mozzarella, pecorino Romano, fragrant freshly-chopped garlic and basil, extra virgin olive oil, and layer of thin, salty, spicy capicollo, or gabagool, if you want to practice your *Sopranos* accent. While I worship at the altar of Amore, Apizza's owner/head pizzaiolo Brian Spangler and crew deftly toss and bake belly-pleasing pies a'plenty, like the house-smoked bacon lined Bacon Bianca, classic tomato and basil topped Apizza 'Margherita, and zesty Tre Colori, layered with tomato walnut pesto, ricotta and thinly-sliced jalapeños. And the house Caesar salad is a must—crisp whole romaine heart leaves sheathed in garlicky housemade dressing and draped with anchovy fillets (be sure to pack breath mints if you're planning to get Amore-ous later).

Packing a big boisterous Italian-American family? Bring everyone along—high-backed booths neatly encapsulate larger parties, while plenty of tables for two appease those seeking more intimate seating. NYC transplants afraid of being let down by the Apizza Scholls hype, fear not—even pizza guru Ed Levine gushed that his visit placed him "in the presence of pizza greatness." And while the aforementioned hype coupled with the regulars' devotion can mean lengthy waits for a table, thankfully the affordable, mostly Italian wine list and well-rounded beer selection make the wait bearable enough that you don't feel the urge to send your competition to swim with the fishes.

MUST EATS

Caesar salad, veggie plate, Apizza Amore, New York White Pie, Meatball Pizza

SIDE DISH

Apizza Scholls accommodates to-go orders Monday through Thursday, but you must walk in and place your order (no phone orders allowed). The wait for your pie-to-go is usually around a half hour, and if you feel like something more potent than a glass of Pinot Grigio or a pint of Caldera Amber Ale in the interim, go across the street to Space Room Lounge for a stiff (and cheap) pour. I recommend the Purple Alien, if you like sneaky-strong cocktails that taste like a grape Skittle.

DETAILS	HOURS
• Reservations accepted via phone or *opentable.com*	DAILY 5-9:30pm
• Street parking is free and generally easy to find	

. . . .

4741 SE HAWTHORNE BOULEVARD
503.233.1286 • *apizzascholls.com*

. . . .

**$$**$$ *Credit Cards Accepted*

ATAULA

TAPAS *in the* **ALPHABET DISTRICT**

Watching the famous Portland swifts flutter madly around the Chapman Elementary chimney in their trademark black pepper-esque vortex, presumably playing truth or dare until someone *finally* takes their wingman's dare to be the first one to dive into the sooty communal bedroom, all I could think about was…I wonder what swift canelones taste like? You could hardly blame me for having canelones on my mind, after all, I was only a scant six blocks from Ataula (more like three as the swift flies), and once you've had Barcelona-born chef/owner Jose Chesa's version—organic chicken braised with tomatoes, shallots and herbs, ground and rolled into homemade tortillas, then smothered in lush rostit sauce and Parmesan béchamel and baked to order in a small cast iron skillet—they're imprinted on your bird brain.

From the moment you touch down in this cheerful Northwest tapas bar and are served your first glass of sangria—lent considerable complexity thanks to a fruit and brandy sous vide—you realize something bueno is about to happen here, in this bright, breezy, wood beam crossed space, open and welcoming like a wide grin, dotted with vivid abstract art and fresh flowers and lorded over by skylights that make the room glow long into the evening in summer. Over in the bar, behind the gently winding white concrete bar dabbed with bits of sparkling sea glass like the Spanish beach you spend most of your workday wishing you were at, porrons and bottles of crisp Basque cider wave a muleta at your sobriety, while the seasonal tapas menu provides heaps of hot, blistered pimientos de padron, smooth white globes of burrata dripping with Spanish tapenade and confit tomatoes, a rich, salty Dungeness crab and potato salad tucked into a repurposed anchovy tin, and a fist-sized hunk of fall-apart tender lamb shoulder surrounded by peach coulis and Catalan beans. Then there's the paella—a pan for two filled with bomba rice, prawns, mussels, calamari, clams, saffron picada and rich, fragrant lobster fume, and bearing a respectable soccarat. Come to think of it, I wonder what swift paella tastes like...just *kidding*!

MUST EATS

Octopus carpaccio, Dungeness crab and potato salad, lamb shoulder with Catalan beans, calamares negros, crema catalana-filled fritters

SIDE DISH

If you're strategic, you can practically spend your whole weekend at Ataula—they're open until midnight on weekend evenings, and on Sundays, they serve a beautiful brunch with treats like serrano ham croissants, brunch paella and pistachio olive oil financiers.

DETAILS	HOURS
• No reservations	TUE-THU...... 4:30-10pm
• Street parking is free and can be difficult to find	FRI-SAT 4:30pm-12am
	SUN............ 10am-2pm

. . . .

1818 NW 23RD PLACE
503.894.8904 • *ataulapdx.com*

. . . .

**$$$**$ *Credit Cards Accepted*

AVA GENE'S

ITALIAN *in* RICHMOND

Slipping into this red leather banquette-lined Division Street trattoria for a night of razzle dazzle dining, it's easy to get swept up in the mirrored and marbled decadence of it all. A round of Love Makes You Feel Ten Feet Tall cocktails to start! Bring on the burrata! Chicken liver pane, a Wagyu culotte, the pork steak for two and a bottle of 1989 Braida Barbera d'Asti, yes please!

But hold on there for a second, big eater, because it would be a crime against the contorni to skirt the greenest pastures of Ava Gene's walnut-hued menu—the plant-based bits. Revel in all the Giardini region has to offer, and soon your table will be honeycombed with small white bowls of pine nut sprinkled pole beans, cauliflower and pickled cherries, sugar snap peas with purslane, and plates of "Tuscan Cavalry" kale salad dusted with SarVecchio Parmesan and crispy golden crumbs of filone baked next door in the ovens of sister bakery Roman Candle.

Post vegetable flurry, in those languid moments between the orecchiette with pork sausage and spring onions and orange zest pistachio cannolo, treat yourself to a mini Italian culinary vocabulary lesson courtesy of the glossary printed in the southeast corner of the menu—a thoughtful touch that saves you from exceeding your smart phone's monthly data allowance googling *colatura* and *affettati*. Which means you can afford a glass of one of the exemplary grappas tucked behind the bar, or perhaps just another order of the chocolate brioche with peanut gelato.

MUST EATS

Raw kale salad, chicken livers pane, pole beans with egg, orecchiette with pork sausage, orange pistachio cannolo

SIDE DISH

Ava Gene's equally marble-endowed next door sidekick, Roman Candle Baking Company, both supplies the pastries for owner/ Stumptown baron Duane Sorenson's coffeehouses *and* serves breakfast, lunch, and a pizza bianca-centric dinner menu from 7am to 10pm daily. So if you're regretting not having ordered that second dessert at Ava Gene's but already relinquished your table, approximately 10 steps and one dark chocolate raspberry torta will take care of that.

DETAILS

+ Reservations accepted via phone or *opentable.com*
+ Street parking is free and generally easy to find

HOURS

DAILY............5-11pm

. . . .

3377 SE DIVISION STREET

971.229.0571 ✦ *avagenes.com*

. . . .

$$$$ *Credit Cards Accepted*

AVIARY

ASIAN in VERNON

Of all the herbs, basil reigns supreme in my book, and if I had my way, all the major advertising slogans would be rewritten to reflect and propagate its glory—*Got Basil? I sure hope so. There's always room for basil. Too true. Pardon me, but do you have any basil? Right here in my handbag. Where's the basil?* At Aviary!

Of course, lest basil steal the (kaffir) limelight, they harness a whole stable of herbs and spices at this sleek Alberta Street nest, one of the most adventurous tables in town, where seriously credentialed kitchen trio Sarah Pliner, Jasper Shen and Kat Whitehead sling exotic, eclectic Asian-inspired small plates that delight and sometimes confound even the most seasoned palate. Chilled zucchini soup comes with bitter almond and chocolate mint, pan-fried sweetbreads are paired with daylilies and water chestnut gremolata, and the butternut squash charlotte is accessorized with fennel and black garlic—the entire menu is a study in "who'd have thunk it?" combinations that are both revelation and education. And never bypass dessert here, not only are they sweet works of art, but they arrive accented with everything from cilantro flowers to, yes, tiny, perfect clippings of bright green Thai basil, like the one tucked into the cluster of fat blackberries topping a summery bourbon panna cotta.

Back in the bar, a sizeable but serene spot to take advantage of Aviary's substantial weeknight happy hour, you can cap off a tough day with a game of cribbage and tobacco bitters-laced Surgeon General's Warning cocktail, or perhaps a refreshing Milkplus Vellocet made with cantaloupe, lime and mint—such a complementary combination, you won't even have to say *I can't believe it's not basil!*

MUST EATS

Heirloom tomato French toast, tempura green beans, butternut squash charlotte, red curry-braised goat, bourbon panna cotta

SIDE DISH

To give you a reason to live through the first workday of the week, Aviary hosts "Classy Monday" in their roomy back bar, which means the $5 slaw dog and Old German tall boy happy hour special runs all night long.

DETAILS

+ Reservations accepted via phone or *opentable.com*
+ Street parking is free and generally easy to find

HOURS

MON-THU	5-10pm
FRI-SAT	5-11pm
Happy Hour	
MON-FRI	5-7pm

1733 NE ALBERTA STREET
503.287.2400 • *aviarypdx.com*

$$$$ *Credit Cards Accepted*

BAMBOO SUSHI

JAPANESE *in the* ALPHABET DISTRICT/KERNS

Once in a bluefish moon, my Monterey Bay Aquarium Seafood Watch card goes through the wash and while waiting for a replacement, I live in terror of committing a sustainability faux pas every time I belly up to a sushi bar. So it's a relief to rest assured that at Bamboo Sushi, I can leave Mr. Guilt to sulk in the Prius during dinner, because my skinless finless fare comes with the finest eco-pedigree around.

Under the scrupulous guidance and vision of owner Kristofor Lofgren, this Japanese restaurant has earned the impressive distinction of being the first certified, sustainable sushi restaurant in the universe as we know it, an accolade that does green-loving Portland proud. Behind the bar, adroit chefs slice flawless sashimi, craft comely sushi rolls, and prepare sophisticated cooked dishes like the grilled hanger steak with Asian mustard mushrooms, kabocha squash tempura, crisp, creamy Alaskan black cod with smoked soy and roasted garlic glaze, and showstopping "house on fire" mackerel, which arrives in a bamboo steamer, suspended over gently smoking alder wood chips.

Apparently, pretty much everyone loves Bamboo Sushi–both locations are perpetually packed with attractive couples and spirited groups of diners socializing and sipping assiduously-selected artisanal sakes, shochu, and lychee martinis with their reproachless dinner catch—so be prepared to wait for a table.

MUST EATS

Grilled shishito peppers with miso butter and bacon, "house on fire" mackerel, black cod, Salmon Nation roll, chocolate egg rolls

SIDE DISH

If you like pleasant surprises, opt for omakase at the sushi bar, where you can watch Bamboo's skilled chefs work their magic.

DETAILS	HOURS
• Reservations are accepted for parties of 7+ nightly at the NW location, and Sun-Thu for parties of 7+ at the SE location	*NW Location* DAILY . . . . 5-10pm *Happy Hour* MON-FRI . . . . 5-6pm *SE Location* DAILY 4:30-10pm
• Street parking is free and generally easy to find at SE, difficult to find at NW	*Happy Hour* MON-FRI 4:30-6pm

. . . .

836 NW 23RD AVENUE • 971.229.1925

310 SE 28TH AVENUE • 503.232.5255

bamboosushi.com

. . . .

**$$$**$ *Credit Cards Accepted*

BAR AVIGNON

NEW AMERICAN *in* HOSFORD-ABERNETHY

This classy little Southeast wine bar is equally charming in the warmest of times and the coldest of times, and considering that we have far more of the latter than the former here in Portland, one of my favorite fall, winter and spring pastimes is to curl up in one of Bar Avignon's cozy black booths with someone special, wistfully sipping rosé and watching the rain pelt the front windows.

Under the watchful eye of owner Nancy Hunt, former bar manager of the late Café Azul, the bar shakes and stirs consistently excellent cocktails, and the wine list is beautifully curated and always intriguing, not surprising considering co-owner Randy Goodman once reigned as iconic Wildwood's longtime wine director. Pair your libations with a dozen plump, briny Kusshi oysters or a mix-and-match artisan cheese and charcuterie board, as an appetite-whetting preamble to chef Eric Joppie's Mediterranean-influenced dinner menu. Cheekily categorized as "for sharing–or not," small plates include melon and cucumber salad with creamy labneh, autumn vegetables with chanterelles and fig walnut salsa, and Washington mussels bathed in a rich tarragon-infused cream sauce that was born to be sopped up with fresh baguette from nearby Little T American Baker, while a handful of hearty mains like roast chicken with braised baby artichokes, duck and pork belly-stuffed cassoulet, and a cod, clam and calamari-choked seafood stew warm weary bones on a frigid night.

Bar Avignon's happy hour makes it disconcertingly easy to arrive at 5pm for the $4 cheese plate and $6 rosé of the day and somehow end up sipping and nibbling until last call, because once you're ensconced in a cushy booth and under this beguiling bar's spell, it's rather painful to return to the real world.

MUST EATS

Bourbon caramel popcorn, cheese board, mussels in tarragon cream, roasted chicken, mud pie sundae

SIDE DISH

Back when I used to co-host a monthly supper club, Table For Twelve, we had one of our most memorable dinners at Bar Avignon, which can accommodate groups of up to 12 at the semi-private back table. Hemmed in on all sides by cases and racks of wine, it's an oenephile's ultimate party setting.

DETAILS	HOURS
• Reservations accepted for groups of up to 12 for the semi-private back table	MON-THU 5-10pm
	FRI-SAT 5pm-12am
	SUN 5-9pm
• Street parking is free and generally easy to find	*Happy Hour*
	MON-FRI 5-6pm

. . . .

2138 SE DIVISION STREET
503.517.0808 • *baravignon.com*

. . . .

**$$$**$ *Credit Cards Accepted*

BEAST

FRENCH *in* CONCORDIA

Intensely-driven, food-obsessed, self-taught chef Naomi Pomeroy has been captivating Portland food lovers for over a decade now, first with her Ripe empire (Family Supper, Clarklewis and Gotham Building Tavern), and now with Beast, a most excellent value for your communal dining buck and still one of Portland's hottest dining tickets six years in.

Pomeroy, who describes her food as simple, refined and feminine, has been lauded by the likes of *Esquire*, *Time*, *The New Yorker*, *GQ*, *Bon Appétit* and *Food & Wine*, was a James Beard Award Best Chef finalist, has been both an Iron Chef and Top Chef, and perhaps most importantly, retains a loyal local following.

Each course on the locally-sourced, lovingly-prepared six-course prix fixe menu is crafted by Pomeroy and sous chef Mika Paredes in Beast's intimate open kitchen, mere feet from the two wooden farmhouse tables that comprise the entirety of the diminutive restaurant's family-style seating. Courses change weekly, and dinner might include chilled watermelon soup to start, followed by Riesling-braised pork belly with green tomato confiture, a cheese plate compiled by noted local cheesemonger Steve Jones, a Charentais melon and radicchio salad, and sour cherry and brown butter cobbler with lemon verbena ice cream.

The only constant on the menu is the charcuterie plate, and even though I've had it many times, it still feels like Christmas when it's set on the table, each comely canapé a bite-sized gift—particularly the foie gras bon bon and chicken liver mousse with candied bacon. Wine lovers, don't pass up the wine pairing—it's a steal at $35 for six pours. You'll leave wishing you could dine this well with your new extended family every night.

MUST EATS
Whatever's on the menu!

SIDE DISH
Across the street from Beast sits hip, sultry Expatriate cocktail lounge, a collaboration between Pomeroy and acclaimed bartender Kyle Linden Webster. Pop in pre/post dinner (or anytime) for expertly mixed drinks, exotic Southeast Asian and Indian inspired drinking snacks, and dessert, like the coconut-glazed strawberry-filled doughnut with black sesame ice cream.

DETAILS	HOURS
• Reservations accepted via phone or *opentable.com*	*Dinner Seatings*
	WED-SAT . . 6pm & 8:45pm
• Street parking is free and generally easy to find	SUN 7pm
	Brunch Seatings
	SUN . . . . 10am & 12pm

. . . .

5425 NE 30TH AVENUE
503.841.6968 • *beastpdx.com*

. . . .

$$$$ *Credit Cards Accepted*

BIWA

JAPANESE *in* BUCKMAN

Whenever I ask a great Portland chef where they hang out after a long night behind a hot stove, almost without fail, Gabe Rosen and Kina Voelz's spunky little izakaya is at the top of their list.

It could be the location—approaching the softly glowing windows that illuminate a dark, deserted street in the Southeast industrial district, you feel like you've discovered a secret hideaway, yet it's just steps from Portland dining hotspots like Le Pigeon, Taqueria Nueve, Cyril's and Simpatica Dining Hall. Perhaps it's the ambiance—there's something distinctly comforting about the sunken basement dining room, with its smooth concrete floors, warm wood paneling, romantic lighting, and bustling galley kitchen.

Maybe it's Biwa's loveable food—grilled hanger steak, chicken heart, and shiitake mushroom skewers dripping with savory juices, deep bowls of ramen with shoyu egg and miso pork loin that flood your mouth with umami, melt-in-your mouth tofu made by nearby Ota Tofu, and crunchy Japanese-style fried chicken. Or, it could be the drink list—Sapporo is on tap, the sake and shochu selection is one of the best in town (try *all* the shochu highballs), and classic cocktails are given a bold tweak to create exotic hybrids like the ginger gimlet, sparkling Negroni, and ginseng Manhattan.

Or, it might just be the classic "all of the above."

MUST EATS

Beef tartare with quail egg, Japanese-style potato salad, asparagus in dashi, lamb skewers, toasted rice soup with hamachi

SIDE DISH

If you're having trouble making tough ordering choices, throw up your hands (put your chopsticks down first) and cry "Omakase!" Or just tell your server in a normal voice that you'd like the $35 chef's choice dinner ($25 beverage pairing optional).

DETAILS

- No reservations
- Street parking is free and easy to find

HOURS

DAILY.......... 5pm-12am

Happy Hour

SUN-THU . 5-6pm & 9-10pm
FRI-SAT... 5-6pm & 9-11pm

. . . .

215 SE 9TH AVENUE
503.239.8830 • *biwarestaurant.com*

. . . .

**$**$$$ *Credit Cards Accepted*

BLUEHOUR

NEW AMERICAN *in the* PEARL DISTRICT

Every so often, we all want to feel like a Lady Who Lunches. You know—oozing old money, the kind of skinny only achieved with the help of a live-in personal trainer, dressed to the nines, and tucked under a white linen napkin come noon on a weekday.

When such an urge strikes, I put on my best Chanel suit (the one I found at the Burnside Goodwill), walk up into the West Hills, stand in front of my favorite mansion, and call a cab to take me to ever so stylish Bluehour, where I sashay into the swanky chandelier-strung dining room, order a dirty martini and the three-course prix fixe Bluehour Plate Special. I eavesdrop on the suited up power lunchers, watch the fashionable Pearl District foot traffic, take the roundabout way to the loo to get a good long look at the oh-so-elegant cheese cart, and dream of returning come nightfall for oysters with cucumber and vermouth mignonette, beef tartare, gnocchi with chanterelles, and peach pistachio clafoutis by candlelight.

It's an indulgence to be sure, particularly when you factor in the cab fare, but a lady who lunches never looks at prices, and besides, Visa bills are so much more fun when they aren't opened. I'm sure the always-gracious staff sees right through me, as a real Lady Who Lunches probably wouldn't drop halibut cheeks on her Chanel suit, nor would she likely order two desserts and drink three martinis and then check her phone in a panic, mumble something about being fired for taking another three-hour lunch break, and dash out the door...but they kindly never let on.

MUST EATS

Beef tartare, Oregon black cod and Tarbais beans, gnocchi with chanterelles and Robiola, chocolate torte, cheese flight

SIDE DISH

You wouldn't think it from the way your wallet starts to quiver upon spying this vision of dining decadence, but Bluehour has one of the best happy hours in town. So dress to impress and take that hot date, then make like Cinderella when last happy hour call tolls at 6:30pm.

DETAILS	HOURS
• Reservations accepted via phone or *opentable.com*	MON-WED. 11:30am-10pm
	THU 11:30am-11pm
• Street parking is metered and can be difficult to find	FRI......... 11:30am-12am
	SAT 5pm-12am
	Happy Hour
	MON-FRI 4-6:30pm
	SAT 5-6:30pm

. . . .

250 NW 13TH AVENUE

503.226.3394 • *bluehouronline.com*

. . . .

$$$$ *Credit Cards Accepted*

BLUEPLATE

AMERICAN *in* DOWNTOWN

The instant Portland's famously weepy skies cloud over and rain begins to pelt the windows, my Pavlovian response is to crave Blueplate's warm 'n melty grilled cheese sandwich dipped in piping hot tomato soup…and a thick chocolate peanut butter shake made with ultra-creamy Cascade Glacier ice cream. A calorically-modest meal it is not, but there's simply nothing more gratifying on a wintry afternoon.

Blueplate chef/owner Jeffery Reiter isn't just cooking up supremely satisfying comfort food, he's providing a nostalgic haven—a classic little soda fountain with a scuffed wood bar, hodge podge of affectionately mismatched booths and tables, eponymous daily specials of mid-20th century lunch counter lore with a Pacific Northwest twist (think grilled meatloaf sandwiches on Texas toast with fresh basil mayo), and vintage glass jars of old-time sweets like root beer barrels, Sweet Tarts and Mary Janes that will send you back to the office with bulging pockets and a guilty candy-eatin' grin.

Tucked into a narrow space in the historic Dekum building along a busy downtown artery, this tiny diner is easy to miss, so watch for the sandwich board perched outside the front door. The menu reads like Mom's home cooking, except my Mom's meatloaf wasn't this rich, her brisket wasn't this tender, her mac 'n cheese did *not* have bacon and mushrooms in it, and she was far more interested in keeping me captive at the table until I ate my salad than inquiring as to whether I'd like a three-scoop caramel apple milkshake, housemade hibiscus and star anise soda, or strawberry ice cream sundae with marshmallow whipped cream and the works for dessert.

MUST EATS

Grilled cheese & tomato soup, Grandma's pot roast, Meatloaf Madness, Northwest sliders, bacon & mushroom mac 'n cheese

SIDE DISH

If you want a mouthwatering preview of your Blueplate experience, click on the homepage's link to the *Diners, Drive-ins and Dives* episode featuring Jeffery making his famous Northwest sliders and mac 'n cheese. You will be riveted, I promise.

DETAILS

+ No reservations
+ Street parking is metered and can be difficult to find

HOURS

MON-FRI 11am-4pm

· ·

308 SW WASHINGTON STREET

503.295.2583 · *eatatblueplate.com*

· ·

$$$$ *Credit Cards Accepted*

29

BOKE BOWL

JAPANESE *in* BUCKMAN

People joke about pork belly being Portland's official food, but I'd venture to say that it's soup, because the only sensible recourse for being chilled to the bone by yet another onslaught of our official precipitation, is re-warming your icy skeleton with rich, nourishing, piping hot soup. So how fitting that Boke Bowl ramen shop serves its beloved soups with pork belly upon request, for those who like to have their soup and eat their pork belly too.

A true Stumptown success story, it only took Brannon Riceci and Patrick Fleming's inner Southeast noodle house a little over a year to evolve from simmering roving ramen pop up to rolling boil of a restaurant. Now, every day when the lunch bell rings, the long communal tables and lone row of two-tops fill up lightning quick, so go early for easy access to chef Fleming's pork brisket-stuffed steam buns, warm Brussels sprouts and cauliflower salad with tofu croutons, kimchi fritters, and unique "Portland-style" ramen lineup that includes the basic pork model plus tasty twists like seafood dashi with olive oil poached shrimp and Rabbit Three Ways—rabbit confit and rabbit meatballs in rabbit dashi.

The shop has earned a large and loyal following, partly due to its excellent product, partly to its welcoming, good-hearted vibes, and partly to its sensitivity to all sorts of slurpers—the marvelous caramelized fennel dashi with Japanese eggplant is vegan (as is the coconut kaffir lemongrass tapioca), gluten free yam noodles can be substituted in any bowl, and there's even a noodle and broth-only Bambino Bowl for the small set, who are further enticed with peanut butter and jelly steam buns, rice tots, lemongrass ginger soft serve, and the mother of all Boke desserts, the soft, spongey homemade twinkies. Which you should never, *ever* only order one of when dining with a group of treacherous coworkers, then turn your back on for even two seconds, because you know when Frank Sinatra warbles "regrets, I've had a few..."? Well, that's exactly the sort of scenario he's talking about.

MUST EATS

Pork belly steam buns, Brussels sprouts and tofu salad, fennel and eggplant ramen, Korean Fried Chicken, Boke twinkies

SIDE DISH

Thursday nights bring "Boke Bird," Boke's weekly Korean Fried Chicken night, which runs from 5 to 9 pm, meaning you may miss part of *X Factor*, but will be home just in time for *Glee*.

DETAILS	HOURS	
• No reservations	MON-WED	11am-3pm
• Street parking is free and can be difficult to find	THU-SUN	11am-9pm
	Boke Bird	
	THU	5-9pm

1028 SE WATER AVENUE
503.719.5698 • *bokebowl.com*

\$\$\$\$ *Credit Cards Accepted*

31

BOLLYWOOD THEATER

INDIAN *in* **VERNON/RICHMOND**

Sitting there with my order number on the table, spicy hot chai or salt lassi in hand, watching the line at this boisterous Indian hotspot's counter grow until it trickles out the door, down the street and around the corner, I always imagine how amazing it would be if everyone who's examining their menu, arguing over whether to get one order of samosas or two, agonizing between the Goan style shrimp or pork vindaloo, and looking longingly at the gently sweating Thums Up colas stuck in the tub of ice at the counter, suddenly burst into a vigorous Bollywood dance number, flash mob style.

This hasn't happened yet, but there's still plenty to look at in the colorful kitsch-crammed dining room, a veritable museum of trinkets and curiosities collected by chef/owner Troy MacLarty on his Indian travels. MacLarty, a Chez Panisse alum, birthed Bollywood to bring the Southern Indian-style street food he'd come to love while living in Berkeley to vada pav-bereft Portland, and residents responded enthusiastically, queueing up patiently for platters of fried okra, kati rolls, and egg masala.

The bright, cheerful and casual restaurant (counter service only and bus your own bhel puri plate) attracts a fascinating cross section of diners—aloo tikki-loving locals, gastrotourists drawn by the favorable media (like the Oregonian's Rising Star 2013 award), and members of the city's Indian-American population seeking the flavors and dishes that remind them of home. The dining room's steady hum means it's just the place to bring adventurous little eaters, and if they act up, although bribery is never (sometimes/usually) the answer, remind them that if they hold it together long enough for you to finish your papri chaat and pint of Kingfisher in peace, there's a trip to neighboring Salt & Straw ice cream shop in order.

MUST EATS

Fried okra, bhel puri, papri chaat, vada pav, kati rolls

SIDE DISH

Buoyed by the unwavering popularity of Bollywood Theater #1, MacLarty is opening a second location in Southeast Portland's D-Street Village (*3010 SE Division St.*) in fall 2013, the grand opening of which he will commemorate with a massive Bollywood dance number in the middle of Division Street. Just kidding, but I'm sure hoping.

DETAILS

- No reservations
- Street parking is free and generally easy to find

HOURS

DAILY 11am-10pm

. . . .

2039 NE ALBERTA STREET

971.200.4711 • *bollywoodtheaterpdx.com*

. . . .

**$$**$$ *Credit Cards Accepted*

BRODER

SCANDINAVIAN *in* HOSFORD-ABERNETHY/ELIOT

During the weekend brunch rush, it is mesmerizing to watch the tight T-shirt-clad Broder boys working the line in this cheerful and sociable Clinton Street café's equally snug kitchen. Calmly and swiftly, they produce a rapid-fire succession of ultra-satisfying Scandinavian dishes like smoking hot cast-iron skillets filled with smoked trout hash and country ham and Gouda scrambles, steaming bowls of buttery porridge, and a never-ending stream of freshly made æbleskiver—pleasantly dense little pancake orbs accompanied by tiny dipping bowls of lemon curd, lingonberry jam and maple syrup.

They also dish up one of my favorite breakfasts in Portland, the Swedish Breakfast Board—a wooden plank loaded with an abbreviated smorgasbord of smoked trout, salami, Swedish farmers cheese, yogurt with honey and seasonal fruit, brown bread, and rye crisp. I'd suggest pairing it with a tart-sweet grapefruit mimosa, to create a breakfast combo well worth abandoning your normal bowl of Rice Krispies.

Although brunch is Broder's big draw, the café serves dinner too, and come the dark nights of winter, there's no cozier place to retreat with a glass of chill-vanquishing Aalborg and an order of Swedish meatballs with sherry cream, a hearty lamb burger, or the four-course Smorgasbord—or all three if you have a Swedish farmer-sized appetite.

MUST EATS

Cardamom roll, smoked trout hash, æbelskiver, Swedish breakfast board, potato pancakes

SIDE DISH

There is a sizeable population of æbleskiver addicts in Portland, so the gods of gravlax and smoked gouda saw fit to bless the opening of Broder Nord, a North Portland sister cafe with the requisite hotsy totsy staff and bottomless bottles of Aquavit.

DETAILS	HOURS
• Reservations accepted via phone for dinner only	DAILY........... 9am-3pm
	WED-SAT.........5-10pm
• Street parking is free and generally easy to find	*Happy Hour*
	WED-SAT 5-6pm

....

2508 SE CLINTON STREET · 503.736.3333

2240 N INTERSTATE AVENUE · 503.282.5555

broderpdx.com

....

**$$**$$ *Credit Cards Accepted*

BUNK SANDWICHES

SANDWICHES *in* BUCKMAN/DOWNTOWN

Tommy Habetz and Nick Wood's lively, scrappy little sandwich shops are bona fide sandwich meccas, as evidenced by the lines out the door come lunchtime. The sammich-loving masses come for the tender, juicy Roast Beef with caramelized onions and horseradish, imposing Pork Belly Cubano, spicy Hot Sausage Po' Boy, classic Oregon Albacore Tuna Melt, simple-but-beautiful Grilled Tillamook Cheddar, and mighty Meatball Parmigiano Hero, the sandwich an incredulous friend once dubbed "a heart attack boat."

They come for the huge sour pickles, red beans and rice, bacon and egg-enhanced potato salad, coconut cream cake, Pie Spot pecan pieholes, Boylan's birch beer, and the Bunk Mimosa–a humble but heady concoction of orange juice and Miller High Life that goes very well with Bunk's bacon, egg and cheese breakfast sandwich. And when every last speck of pork shoulder and tripe and fried mortadella and oxtail confit is gone and all that's left on their red plastic lunch trays is a sprinkling of Kettle Chip crumbs and a few dribbles of Mexican Coke, we, I mean *they*, leave with big sandwich eatin' grins.

MUST EATS

Roast Beef, Meatball Parmigiano Hero, Oregon Albacore Tuna Melt, Italian Cured Meats, BLT

SIDE DISH

If Bunk's closing time is your staggering-out-of-bed time, worry not about Pork Belly Cubano deprivation—just meander down to Bunk *Bar*, located in Portland's industrial waterfront district. A fun, full bar endowed hipster hangout, it's got Bunk's serious sandwich menu plus live music, tater tots, and night owl hours (*1028 SE Water Ave.; weekdays 11am-12am, weekends 11am-1am*).

DETAILS	HOURS
• No reservations	*SE Location*
• Street parking is free and	DAILY 8am-3pm
generally easy to find at SE,	*SW Location*
metered and difficult to find	DAILY 8am-3pm
at the downtown location	

. . . .

621 SE MORRISON STREET • 503.477.9515

211 SW 6TH AVENUE • 503.972.8100

bunksandwiches.com

. . . .

$$$$ *Credit Cards Accepted*

CACAO

CHOCOLATE *in* DOWNTOWN

A must-see for visitors and *the* one-stop shop for any personal chocolate needs you may have, this dazzling downtown chocolate boutique is a temple to the Supreme Bean, with lofty ceilings, marble countertops, gleaming glass display cases, and spotless shelves filled with the handiwork of some of the world's greatest chocolate makers.

Owners Jesse Manis, who spent a decade at acclaimed Seattle chocolatier Fran's before opening his dream shop, and Aubrey Lindley, who has a background in fine arts and design, are the Anna Wintours of haute chocolate, and have amassed a cacao cache that would move an Oompa Loompa to tears— an immaculate collection of handmade bars, bon bons, barks, couverture, truffles and sauces by renowned chocolatiers both national and worldwide, as well as those right here in Portland, like Sarah Hart (Alma Chocolate), David Briggs (Xocolatl de Davíd), and Jeremy Karp (Batch PDX). Non-edible but equally indulgent wares include glossy chocolate books, Aftelier's cacao perfume and luxurious chocolate saffron body oil, and Portland-based 33 Books Co.'s helpful *33 Bars of Chocolate* tasting journals, which have drinking chocolate added to the ink.

Should you prefer your theobromine high in liquid form, indulge in a velvety Caffé Vita mocha, luscious housemade hot chocolate, or one of Cacao's legendary drinking chocolates—melted milk and dark chocolates infused with cinnamon, cayenne, smoked paprika and ginger, the molten results conjuring sensory visions of what the Willy Wonka chocolate river might taste like when you "accidentally" fall in.

MUST EATS

Xocolatl de Davíd's brown butter bar, Batch PDX's spicy passion bon bon, Cocanú's Abeja bar, Rogue's Silvestre bar, Cacao's Spicy Dark Drinking Chocolate

SIDE DISH

Should you find yourself on the south end of downtown with a severe cacao cramp, Cacao has a tiny but impeccably-stocked annex located in the landmark Heathman Hotel (712 SW Salmon St.; 503.274.9510).

DETAILS	HOURS	
• Street parking is metered and can be difficult to find	MON-THU	10am-8pm
	FRI-SAT	10am-10pm
	SUN	11am-6pm

414 SW 13TH AVENUE
503.241.0656 • cacaodrinkchocolate.com

Credit Cards Accepted

CANDY BABEL

CANDY *in* KING

Here in the land of vegan tattoo parlors, palacial urban chicken coops, curbside composting, 3,000-square-foot rooftop restaurant gardens, ballgame burgers made with grass-fed beef, dedicated gluten-free breweries, and tea that comes with a trackable batch number so you can investigate its provenance, it's no surprise that even our sweet shops are conscientious—as evidenced by delightful candy queen Amani Greer's charmingly upstanding Alberta Street sugar shack, land of high-principled lemon meringue malt balls, chocolate-covered blueberries, winegums, mint caramels, Scandinavian salt licorice, sour grapefruits, violet lollipops, and gummies galore.

Amani, whose credo is the dead faint inducing "Try Everything," oversees her stock with a gimlet eye, often importing European candies to avoid the high fructose corn syrup pitfalls of the American versions, stocking gluten-free, dairy-free and vegan treats, and even making her own cotton candy—organic, kosher, free-trade, no-GMO "sweetie puffs" in flavors like cardamom, coconut, rose and watermelon. Nostalgic treats like Zotz, candy buttons, wax lips and licorice pipes share the space with small batch truffles crafted by neighborhood chocolatiers and a dozen different kinds of locally-sourced honey sticks, a row of antique toffee hammers gleam in the glass display case, and handmade piñatas dangle from the ceiling. Should you decide to share your newfound treasures with someone else, no need to deliver them via crumpled white paper bag filled with headless peachy penguins; instead, tuck your bounty securely into one of the beautiful vintage tins that line the entire shop—they are from Amani's own private collection, so they make the quintessential Portland gift, delicious *and* recycled.

MUST EATS

Green apple army men, chicken feet, Finnish licorice, coconut cotton candy, Marushka truffles

SIDE DISH

Amani will roll her cotton-candy-machine-for-hire right into your party and spin sugar clouds for guests (choose from 100+ flavors). If your party is French Revolution-themed, she'll even paste pictures of Marie Antoinette's head on the paper cone.

DETAILS	HOURS
• Street parking is free and easy to find	DAILY..........12-6:30pm

. . . .

1219 NE ALBERTA STREET

503.867.0591 • *candybabel.com*

. . . .

$$$$ *Credit Cards Accepted*

CANTEEN

VEGAN *in* SUNNYSIDE

Just stepping inside this hip little Stark Street café makes you feel like a better person—the crisp scent of freshly pulverized greenery fills your lungs with disease-fighting chlorophyll molecules, pitchers of water infused with lemon and cucumber slices refresh your tap water tortured intestines, and the curved marble bar supports overflowing baskets of shiny produce waiting patiently to be sacrificed to the Vitamix gods.

On the liquid side of things, juices range from the affable apple-based Summer Breeze to the garlicky, beet-sweet Super Veggie, which will make your liver stand on end and sing Hallelujah, while easily downable smoothies like the zingy Ginger-Berry hook you on healthy drinking. Solid food is simple and well-prepared—choose from the quinoa, kale and maple tempeh-based Portland Bowl, kimchi and red curry peanut sauce-topped Bangkok Bowl, or the Southern Bowl, a blend of brown rice, Soy Curls, collard greens and black-eyed peas. Of the salads trio, the Quinoa Confetti with crisp apple, raisins, cashews and fresh mint doesn't disappoint, and for dessert, go crazy with the raw cheesecake of the day—it's so good you won't miss the dairy at all, and that's coming from a lactose devotee.

With the exception of the blond wood benches and hanging frames filled with raw apple cider vinegar, sacks of brown basmati rice, and cartons of coconut water, most everything in the cafe is white, so if you've been a very good vegan who has just sustained a sharp blow to the head before stepping inside, you could certainly be forgiven for thinking that you've gone to heaven. Whether or not heaven has kombucha on tap, I can't say, but they definitely have Canteen's "shots" beyond the Pearly Gates, because Red Bull has it all wrong, nothing gives you wings like a straight shot of raw ginger juice or E3Live.

MUST EATS

Tropical Greens smoothie, oatmeal with berries and hazelnuts, cashew cream parfait, Portland Bowl, Quinoa Confetti

SIDE DISH

Canteen proprietor Brian Heck, whose glowing countenance renders him a walking ad for a plant-based diet, also owns the darling snub-nosed Sip juicemobiles, strategically placed to alkalize both the happy hippy crowd pouring into People's Co-op (*3029 SE 21st Ave.*) and the gravy-guzzling sinners staggering out of Pine State Biscuits (*2210 NE Alberta St.*).

DETAILS	HOURS
• No reservations	TUE-SUN 9am-9pm
• Street parking is free and easy to find	

. . . .

2816 SE STARK STREET

503.922.1858 • *canteenpdx.com*

. . . .

$$$$ *Credit Cards Accepted*

CARTOPIA

CART POD *in* BUCKMAN

Cartopia is a Portland landmark all its own; vivacious family-friendly cart pod by day, merrymaker's mirage by night—seven funky food wagons filled with all manner of deliriously good drunk food circled 'round a lumpy stretch of asphalt at the busy corner of SE Hawthorne and SE 12th.

Thanks to its eclectic tenants and their meandering hours, this lively little pod attracts a diverse patronage—families crowd the picnic tables come supper time, angsty tweens share iPods and hot fries and hand pies bought with hoarded lunch money until curfew looms, and the late-night crowd includes everyone from midnight snackers to the tipsy revelers who hold Cartopia sacred as the obligatory midpoint between the bars and their beds. Satay poutine, fried peach handpies, carnitas burritos, wood-fired puttanesca pizzas, shrimp po' boys, Nutella banana crepes, and pumpkin pie PBJs—Cartopia's got it all.

My top destinations are Potato Champion—a charmingly bemuraled cart where perfect-specimen Belgian-style fries come with horseradish ketchup and tarragon anchovy mayo or buried beneath chunky Ellsworth Creamery cheese curds and smothered in gravy to create a heart-stopping (maybe literally) poutine; Whiffies Fried Pies—the ever-popular purveyor of hot, flaky crescents of fried pie goodness filled with everything from barbecue brisket and vegan three-bean chili, to marionberries and coconut pudding; Pyro Pizza—a miracle of engineering with a wood-fired pizza oven actually built inside, enabling the pizzaiolos within to bake authentic thin-crust margherita pizzas in mere minutes, and PBJ's—whose inventive twists on this most revered of American classics might cause your brain to short circuit upon first menu read, so play it safe with the Nutella and raspberry jam-filled Cynthia, or go wild with the Sriracha, fresh basil, curry and marmalade-stuffed Spicy Thai.

MUST EATS

Potato Champion's poutine, Whiffies' chocolate peanut butter creme pie, Pyro Pizza's margherita pizza, PBJ's Hot Hood

SIDE DISH

Street parking around Cartopia is free and can be difficult to find. However desperate you are to get your hands on a fried cherry pie, do not be tempted to park in the alluringly empty lot across SE 12th street, as there is an excellent chance your car will be picked off by a lurking tow truck in mere minutes.

DETAILS

+ Street parking is free and can be difficult to find

HOURS

PBJ's
TUE-SUN 11am-7pm

HOURS CONT.

Potato Champion
TUE-SUN 12pm-3am

Pyro Pizza
TUE-SUN ...... Hours vary

Whiffies
TUE-SUN ...... Hours vary

· ·

SE 12TH & SE HAWTHORNE BOULEVARD

pbjsgrilled.com ✦ *potatochampion.com*
pyropizzacart.com ✦ *whiffies.com*

· ·

$$$$ *Some carts are cash only, ATM on premises*

CASTAGNA

MODERN *in* HOSFORD-ABERNETHY

It's universally known that in Portland, you can wear jeans to anything—work, cocktail parties, your wedding, and by all means, restaurants, be they of the white tablecloth or white paper napkin persuasion. That's just how we roll here in Stumptown, and nobody thinks twice about it, except maybe department stores, as they yet again haul all their wool dress trousers to the sale rack. But there is something about long-time Portland restaurateur Monique Siu's zen-like Hawthorne Boulevard dining room that inspires one to ditch the coffee-stained denim and don their best ModCloth frock or cleanest plaid shirt and corduroy skinny pants, plus special occasion Toms (the silver Glitters, obviously).

Perhaps it's the pristine walls, adorned with a sprig of chestnuts, perhaps it's chef Justin Woodward's pristine modernist cuisine, presented via tasting menus that wind and wend their way through a mélange of arrestingly visual "snacks" like eucalyptus lime emulsion filled buttermilk puffs and dollops of lamb tartare balanced on the end of smooth, pale rib bones, followed by dashi-poached sole and kohlrabi swimming in crawfish geranium bisque and perfect cubes of sanguine, local brewery mash-finished ribeye with Parmesan cream, salsify and baby wild onions. Come dessert, delight in tiny round birch financiers tucked beneath an alabaster tree branch draped with smoked apple leather leaves, followed by a flawless orb of fig leaf and white chocolate ganache coated in dark Valrhona chocolate. It's a wild world of sprigs, twigs, foams and edible landscapes so captivating that when dinner ends, you'll be sorry to click your silver glitter Toms and whisper "There's no place like home."

MUST EATS

The unique, sensual prix fixe menus are oft-changing, so just go with the foams and sprigs flow.

SIDE DISH

Adjoining Café Castagna shares a wall and bathrooms with Castagna, but its joyful din and rustic cuisine are worlds away from its dignified sibling's serene environment, making it a good spot for a low-key dinner or happy hour when you're in the neighborhood. Try the burger, it's famous 'round these parts.

DETAILS	HOURS	
• Reservations accepted via phone or *opentable.com*	WED-THU	5:30-9pm
• Street parking is free and generally easy to find	FRI-SAT	5:30-10pm

· ·

1752 SE HAWTHORNE BOULEVARD

503.231.7373 • *castagnarestaurant.com*

· ·

$$$$ *Credit Cards Accepted*

CHEESE BAR

CHEESE in MT. TABOR

A Cheese Bar visit starts out much like a 12-step program—first, you admit you're powerless over cheese, then you turn yourself over to a higher cheese power (owner/cheesemonger Steve Jones, aka the Cheese Whisperer), and allow him to help you assemble the perfect cheese plate. Add a heap of local Olympic Provisions chorizo, a fresh crusty baguette, a side of pickled vegetables, a bottle of wine or cider, and a piece of chocolate almond date bread pudding, and you have a spiritual Cheese Bar awakening of the most profound kind.

Which is why Portland's wedge and wheel crowd flock from all over the city to this corner of the sleepy Mt. Tabor woods seeking Steve's creamy, dreamy and proudly odoriferous wares, carefully compiled into "soft-ripened," "stinky" and "Neal's Yard"-themed boards, mixed into dips, sliced into ham and Havarti sandwiches and summery Caprese salads, and melted into mac'n cheese. Not just a one-trick cheese pony, Cheese Bar's small but mighty lunch and dinner menu includes meat and pâté boards showcasing local charcutiers, seasonal salads, soups and stratas, and a dessert or two. If you're reluctant to leave your cheese bubble post-feast, linger over the shelves of Three Little Figs jams and Ames Farm honeys, stock up on Xocolatl de Davíd bars, fancy crackers and tinned sardines, even buy a fondue pot or a DIY cheese kit, although really—call me co-dependent, but why would you need to make your own cheese when you have Steve and his glorious Cheese Bar?!

MUST EATS

Neal's Yard cheese board, blue cheese dip, Alpine cheese fondue, mac 'n cheese, roasted eggplant and fresh mozzarella sandwich

SIDE DISH

Steve hosts all sorts of delectable cheese, charcuterie, wine and beer tastings, as well as educationally edible events like his popular wintertime Raclette Wednesdays. To stay updated, sign up for his e-newsletter at the bottom of the Cheese Bar website.

DETAILS

+ No reservations
+ Street parking is free and generally easy to find

HOURS

TUE-SUN 11am-11pm

. . . .

6031 SE BELMONT STREET

503.222.6014 + *cheese-bar.com*

. . . .

**$$**$$ *Credit Cards Accepted*

CHEF NAOKO BENTO CAFÉ

JAPANESE *in* DOWNTOWN

Portland food lovers in the know have a quiet love affair with chef Naoko Tamura's cuisine, and come lunch hour, a loyal contingency of bento-philes fills the cheerful café, a tiny urban oasis dotted with gently swaying white lanterns and accented with leafy plants and fresh produce.

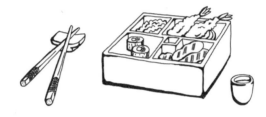

Chef Naoko's commitment to the highest-quality local and organic ingredients and her sense of food artistry are evident in each exquisite black-lacquered bento box that comes out of the kitchen—you won't see any sensational kyaraben-style presentations, just humble and consistently excellent offerings like grilled fish or tofu in a delicately flavorful house ginger teriyaki sauce, Japanese-style fried shrimp, marinated chicken, or grilled tofu, accompanied by pretty piles of bright organic greens, house pickle salad, higiki seaweed with barley, brown rice sprinkled with black sesame seeds, and perhaps a quivering cube of fresh Ota tofu topped with a dollop of inky sweet Japanese miso sauce.

The rice bowls are hearty and delicious, with grilled ground chicken and tofu cakes served atop lightly cooked vegetables and cabbage over steamed rice; an ideal meal when paired with housemade iced tea on a midsummer's day or traditional Japanese roasted tea come winter. The café doubles as sort of a mini-spa for the soul—one of Chef Naoko's delicious meals and a dose of her graciousness is enough to put you in a blissful trance for days.

MUST EATS

Organic miso soup, grilled mochi and cheese, Jefferson bowl, farmers veggie bento, wild salmon ginger bento

SIDE DISH

Chef Naoko runs an extensive catering business from her downtown kitchen, and with adequate notice she can cater all manner of business and group functions—her artful bento is a welcome respite from the same old ordinary meeting food.

DETAILS

- No reservations
- Street parking is metered and generally easy to find

HOURS

TUE-FRI..11:30am-2:30pm
SAT 11:30am-3pm
WED-FRI 6-9:30pm

1237 SW JEFFERSON STREET
503.227.4136 • *chefnaoko.com*

**$$**$$ *Credit Cards Accepted*

CLARKLEWIS

NEW AMERICAN *in* BUCKMAN

Tucked away in a former warehouse in Southeast Portland's industrial district, backed by the Willamette and sharing the still-gritty neighborhood with a handful of intrepid eateries like Olympic Provisions, Bunk Bar, and Boke Bowl, Clarklewis always reminds me of the tents in *Harry Potter*—not much to look at from the outside, but opening up into something magical.

Glossy, polished concrete floors and flickering tea lights glow in the sleek, loft-like dining room, a wood-fired oven sparks in the center of the open kitchen, and well-dressed couples enjoying a sexy date night clink highball glasses at the glammy little bar nestled into the far corner of the dining room. In fair weather, the floor-to-ceiling glass-paneled garage doors that front the restaurant roll up to let a gentle breeze waft thorough the dining room, the ideal setting for a long, blissful summer supper.

In tandem with the dining room's effortless-chic elegance, chef Dolan Lane's rustic French and Italian influenced cuisine has a sophisticated twist and strong Pacific Northwest flair—like the Viridian Farms asparagus salad with wild sorrel and hazelnuts in porcini vinaigrette, spaghetti tossed with prosciutto and Denison Farm fava beans, and hearth-roasted Carlton Farms pork shoulder with savory Oregon cheddar dumplings. And as you nibble the polenta shortcake with Meyer lemon sorbet and huckleberry compote, I think you'll agree—it's what's inside a Harry Potter tent/restaurant that counts.

MUST EATS

Beet salad, wild mushroom arancini, housemade tagliatelle with lamb ragu, ember-roasted pork loin, burger

SIDE DISH

Clarklewis has one of the best happy hours in the city—martinis, gimlets, and house wines are $5, and food specials run the gamut from the $1 olive oil fried almonds to a $3 artisan cheese plate and $5 fennel caraway meatballs. For $6, you can order the hefty oak-grilled Clarklewis burger, a full meal in itself—with the option to gild the burger lily with an egg, pork belly, and/or Oregon blue cheese.

DETAILS

- Reservations accepted via phone and *opentable.com*
- Street parking is free and can be difficult to find

HOURS

MON-FRI..... 11:30am-2pm
MON-THU........ 4:30-9pm
FRI-SAT 4:30-10pm
Happy Hour
MON-SAT.... 4:30-6:30pm

. . . .

1001 SE WATER AVENUE

503.235.2294 • *clarklewispdx.com*

. . . .

$$$$ *Credit Cards Accepted*

CLYDE COMMON

NEW AMERICAN *in* DOWNTOWN

Whenever I'm in the mood to live like a mover 'n shaker for a few hours, I stop by Clyde Common, a bona fide downtown hotspot whose popular-kid hipness is tempered by the laid-back vibe and intriguing yet approachable menu. The cosmopolitan tavern's dining room sports rows of long wooden communal tables teeming with hungry local somebodies rubbing elbows with still unknownbodies, suits chatting up hipsters, locals and foreign-accented guests of the adjoining Ace Hotel dining side by side—all relishing plates of chef Chris DiMinno's whey granita-topped red and green strawberry salad, beet greens and ricotta ravioli, and grilled chicken thighs with bulgur and smoked mushrooms. Pastry chef Danielle Pruett's dessert menu is one of the best in town, so you should definitely also socialize with her chocolate graham tart with butterscotch ice cream and whiskey caramel.

The west side of the stylish, high-ceilinged space is occupied by the boisterous bar, where bar manager Jeffrey Morgenthaler and crew mix and muddle some of the best cocktails around, and maintain a serious whiskey cabinet. Wine director Star Black's list is essentially infallible, so get a bottle of bubbly to share with someone you love, or, in the spirit of the communal atmosphere, with someone you just met. If you're tired of being besieged for your autograph or desire an intimate conversation with your new champagne friend over a piece of blueberry crumb cake with chèvre anglaise and peach cream, request a table upstairs in the more private, albeit not much quieter, loft.

MUST EATS

Charcuterie board, squid ink fideo, cavatelli with braised rabbit, chicken and bulgur, chocolate tart with butterscotch ice cream

SIDE DISH

On weekends, Clyde serves brunch, and what a brunch it is. Recover from the previous evening's shenanigans with a Brandy Milk Punch or Clamato-fortified Caesar, then dive into biscuits and gravy with roasted garlic sausage, the bacon marmalade-slathered club sandwich, and jojos with béarnaise. For extra credit, try and figure out which seat at the bar has the best view of bar manager Jeffrey Morgenthaler's renowned tushie.

DETAILS
- Reservations accepted via phone for parties of 6-12
- Street parking is metered and can be difficult to find

HOURS
MON-THU . 11:30am-12am
FRI 11:30am-1am
SAT 9am-1am
SUN 9am-11pm
Happy Hour
DAILY 3-6pm

. . . .

1014 SW STARK STREET
503.228.3333 • *clydecommon.com*

. . . .

**$$$**$ *Credit Cards Accepted*

THE COUNTRY CAT

AMERICAN *in* MONTAVILLA

Strolling the stretch of Southeast Stark Street between 82nd and Mt. Tabor, I'm crushing on spunky Montavilla, a big city neighborhood even a small towner would feel at home in. The all-American lineup of small businesses occupying its seven-block commercial core include the neighborhood mechanic, lumber store, Academy movie theater, pizzeria, pie shop, bakery, requisite handful of dive bars, and The Country Cat, a humble but dapper family-friendly little eatery woven seamlessly into Montavilla's working-class tapestry.

Chef/owner Adam Sappington's Midwestern upbringing, longtime tour of kitchen duty at renowned Wildwood restaurant, and deep affection for Portland's edible resources influence his farm-to-table country-cookin'-with-an-edge. Order the cast iron skillet fried chicken with bacon-braised collards or get a bit fancier with the hickory-smoked duck leg in porcini mustard, grilled Idaho trout, and roasted sweet pepper hash. And then there's the infamous Whole Hog—a porkfecta of rolled belly, grilled ham steak and smoked shoulder with South Carolina grits.

Pastry chef/other half Jackie Sappington rides herd on a dessert menu that elevates classics to new levels—her cheesecake is laced with bourbon and tucked into a dark chocolate crust, her fruit crisp is baked with sweet local plums and brown sugar and paired with creamy butter pecan ice cream, and her take on good old-fashioned pudding involves three tea party-sized cups of chocolate, butterscotch and crème brûlée—always a hit with kids and kids at heart alike.

MUST EATS

Cinnamon rolls (weekends only), lemon poppyseed challah French toast, skillet-fried chicken, Whole Hog, pudding trio

SIDE DISH

Doing their neighborhood and city a great service, The Country Cat serves brunch daily starting at 9am, so you never have to think twice about what day it is when you're craving smoked steelhead Benedict and chicken-fried steak for breakfast.

DETAILS	HOURS
• Reservations can be made via phone or *opentable.com*	DAILY . . . . 9am-2pm 5pm-9pm
• Street parking is free and generally easy to find	

. . . .

7937 SE STARK STREET
503.408.1414 • *thecountrycat.net*

. . . .

**$$$**$ *Credit Cards Accepted*

CYRIL'S

WINE & CHEESE *in* BUCKMAN

In the beginning, the wine gods created wineries. Then they created wineries with built-in wine bars, and then when they were good and jolly-tipsy, they created wineries with built-in wine bars with cheese counters curated by former Murray's Cheese affineurs/American Cheese Society board members who author books like *The Guide to West Coast Cheese* and *The Cheesemaker's Apprentice* in their spare time. And at that point, everyone was like, hey, who needs light?!

Well, nobody at this sexy little inner Southeast winery-wine bar-fromagerie, where low-slung chandeliers and votives emit just enough of a glow to allow you to choose from the two dozen-or-so glass pours and admire your slate plate of Vendéen Bichonné and Abbaye de Belloc. Where the secret, sunny back patio paired with a bottle of something summery might cause you to accidentally spend an entire Saturday afternoon sipping rosé and eating goat gouda. Where a small, succinct cheese case peddles wheels of washed rinds, sticks of charcuterie, and small, perfect bundles of burrata, next to a tightly-curated collection of cheese-friendly snacks like Beecher's crackers and Jacobsen salt and Chunky Pig caramel corn. And where Clay Pigeon

Winery winemaker Michael Claypool and cheesemonger Sasha Davies preside deliciously over their respective passions, uniting them on a well-rounded menu that besides fine wine and cheese, highlights simple, satisfying foods like plump, warm blue cheese gougères, rich Monger's mac 'n cheese, feta-studded farro and lentil salads, and summer vegetable tarts with feathery butter crusts. And the wine gods saw that all of the above was good.

MUST EATS

Cheese board, gougères, chickpea carrot salad, stuffed flank steak, made-to-order ice cream sandwiches

SIDE DISH

For those who like to help good causes, particularly ones involving cheese, Cyril's has a monthly CSC (Community Supported Cheese) club. Davies chooses a wheel of something divine and puts shares of it up for grabs on Kickstarter, then local cheese lovers unite to buy it, fetching their allotment at the ensuing cheese and wine party.

DETAILS	HOURS
• No reservations	MON-SAT . . . . . Hours vary
• Street parking is free and easy to find	*Happy Hour*
	MON-SAT 4-6pm

. . . .

815 SE OAK STREET
503.206.7862 • *cyrilspdx.com*

. . . .

**$$**$$ *Credit Cards Accepted*

DAR SALAM

MIDDLE EASTERN *in* CONCORDIA

If a picture says a thousand words, then Dar Salam's walls are serious chatterboxes, because the other day, in the brief lull between my sumac-dusted romaine salad and lamb shawarma platter, I counted nearly 150 photos hanging on them. Which equals roughly as many words as there are grains of basmati rice beneath your marga. It's the *War and Peace* of walls! Speaking of which, if the only images that spring to mind when someone mentions Iraq are morose and disquieting, let this infallibly gracious Alberta Street eatery give you a new Middle Eastern mindset, via the greatest of international unifiers—a delicious home-cooked feast. It's the United Nations of meals.

Separated by the war, the two Baghdad-born best friends who own Dar Salam, Ghaith Sahib and Maath Hamed, both ended up in Portland via a difficult, roundabout journey, then teamed up to open a restaurant serving the authentic dishes of their homeland. Passing through the twinkle light and rosemary bush-framed patio and into the charming turn-of-the-century converted carriage house, you're enveloped by walls the color of turmeric, nearly every inch hung with photos depicting the art and architecture of Iraq, alongside pictures of Sahib's and Hamed's families. A flat screen television above the hookah-topped back bar flashes vivid, peaceful scenes of the Tigris and Euphrates rivers, families splashing along the banks of Habbaniyah Lake, white-robed Iraqi fisherman at work, sheep herders guiding flocks through the lush pastures of Kurdistan, and Bagdad street vendors peddling stacks of fresh-baked flatbread, pickles and tea. Lilting, hypnotic Middle Eastern music plays as you dig into pickled mango salad, baked onions stuffed with coriander, cumin and pomegranate-molasses-soaked rice, and platters striped with tender lamb shawarma over basmati rice, thick, ruddy chickpea tomato stew, and creamy tzatziki with cucumbers. It's the sort of spot where you tend to stay awhile, sipping cardamom-spiked Arab coffee and eating baklava, listening to the walls ramble on while you read the *War and Peace* CliffsNotes.

MUST EATS

Iraqi dolma, pickled mango salad, marga, shawarma, baklava

SIDE DISH

The black and red Aladdin's Castle Café sign over the bar is a nostalgic nod to the Sahib family's first venture, a Middle Eastern food cart whose success set the foundation for Dar Salam.

DETAILS	HOURS
• No reservations	MON-FRI ... 11am-2:30pm
• Street parking is free and generally easy to find	.... 4:30-10pm
	SAT 11am-10pm
	Happy Hour
	MON-FRI 4:30-6pm

2921 NE ALBERTA STREET

503.206.6148 • *darsalamportland.com*

**$$**$$ *Credit Cards Accepted*

DIN DIN

FRENCH *in* KERNS

Every Sunday morning, I lie in bed imagining the mind-blowing Sunday brunch I'm going to conjure up. In my imagination, this spread somewhat resembles a Heston Blumenthal extravaganza, but when reality taps me politely on the shoulder at around 11am asking if I'm planning to put down *Heston's Fantastical Feasts* and start prepping the lamb crepinette, my resolve has gone out the window. But not all is lost, for it's possible to imagine a glorious Sunday brunch and eat it too, without having to do a single dish, courtesy of chef Courtney Sproule and her delightful Din Din.

Courtney, a self-taught cook and protégé of Portland's Chef Studio's beloved late founder Robert Reynolds, first came to fame with her pop up supper club, breathtaking multi-course communal suppers in unusual, whimsically-decorated settings all over the city—a terrarium shop's lush overgrown gardens one night, a charming church nave the next. Then, in spring 2013, Courtney found a permanent nest for her mobile feasts, a small, exquisite space hidden in the depths of the inner Northeast industrial district, where she now serves stationary but just as artfully-themed weekend suppers, a light breakfast and lunch "Fee Fee" menu on weekdays, and the aforementioned decadent Sunday "Matinée" brunch. All of which require zero dish-washing. And *that* is what you call a Din Din win-win.

MUST EATS

Soft-boiled egg with candied tomato, spice cake with cheese, ham and honey, duck egg omelette, lamb crepinette, hazelnut shortbread

SIDE DISH

If you can't make it to the weekend extravaganza, simply must have a preview, or just want to dip your toe into the Din Din waters, pop in for the Thursday cocktail hour (4-8pm)—you can sip crémant and Champs-Élysées cocktails, nibble cheese and piment d'Espelette hazelnuts, and order a la carte dishes from the weekend supper menu.

DETAILS

+ Reservations accepted via phone or email
+ Street parking is free and easy to find

HOURS

Fee Fee Café Menu
MON-FRI ..7:30am-5:30pm
Din Din Suppers
THU 7pm
FRI-SAT 7:30pm
Sunday Matinée Brunch
SUN............10am-3pm

. . . .

920 NE GLISAN STREET

971.544.1350 ✦ *dindinportland.com*

. . . .

$$ - $$$$ *Credit Cards Accepted*

DOC

ITALIAN *in* CONCORDIA

DOC is such a fetching space, you may forget to pay attention to your date because you're so smitten with the captivatingly romantic little gingham curtain framed dining room. Once you're able to focus on the fine meal ahead of you, test your companion's culinary savvy by making him/her interpret chef Jobie Bailey's cryptically-written dish descriptions, like the *pole bean, peach, raspberry, crottin* and *cavatelli, lamb shank, chickweed.*

If he/she in turn tries to test your wine finesse by requesting that you choose the bottle, just smile smugly and pick the first thing that catches your eye, because this beautifully constructed Italian-only wine list is foolproof. Hold hands while you sip Prosecco, feed each other bites of creamy lobster mushroom risotto, nibble plum-glazed lamb ribs and then lick each other's fingers clean. Er, maybe that's taking it too far. Lick your own fingers clean and then order the sweet cream panna cotta and olive oil cake with chocolate sorbet.

However romantic you're feeling by the time sommelier extraordinaire Austin Bridges helps you choose the ideal Moscato d'Asti or grappa digestif, I suggest that you do not make out in the bathroom, for the door is right smack in the center of the dining room and if you've had too many of DOC's exceptional Negronis and forgot to lock it behind you, nobody will find it very romantic at all when you, your Spanx, and your lipstick-smeared date are revealed in all their glory.

MUST EATS

Oysters with black pepper and vodka mignonette, kale hazlenut risotto, ricotta gnudi with chanterelles, albacore, panna cotta

SIDE DISH

Next door lies pretty Nonna, DOC's casual counterpart, a homey little trattoria and wine bar focusing on Italian-inspired small plates and great wine, and yet another delicious project by visionary local developer and neighborhood resident Dayna McErlean, who also owns the excellent Yakuza izakaya just up the street. For a weekend getaway in gastronomically-gifted Concordia, book McErlean's Kuza Cabin, a chic, cozy carriage-house-turned-studio tucked away in the back of Yakuza's serene Japanese garden (details at www.vrbo.com/375245).

DETAILS

- Reservations can be made via phone or *opentable.com*
- Street parking is free and generally easy to find

HOURS

TUE-SAT 6-10pm

. . . .

5519 NE 30TH AVENUE

503.946.8592 • *docpdx.com*

. . . .

$$$$ *Credit Cards Accepted*

DOUBLE DRAGON

VIETNAMESE *in* HOSFORD-ABERNETHY

Normally, I stand firmly in the camp of waste not, want not, but I cannot tell a lie—many, *many* napkins were harmed in the making of this story. It's inevitable, because when this hip Southeast sandwich joint slings a pork belly, roast duck, or heaven help you, its beef and pork meatball monstrosity onto the pickup counter, you best head straight for the napkin dispenser—or better yet, get everything to go and eat at home in the shower.

In the kitchen, chef/owner Rob Walls, a Momofuku and Bunk Sandwiches alum and self-proclaimed "white fellow from NJ," crafts Vietnamese-inspired riffs on the traditional banh mi, with soft, supple rolls in place of crisp baguettes, and local, sustainably-raised pork, beef and poultry in place of the mystery meat. These ham-fisted sandwich hybrids dwarf the small tin plates they're served on, and once in hand, they drip, crunch, squish, gush, and then, somehow, disappear—call it a banh mi blackout, call it superhuman gustatory grace in the face of gastro-adversity; whatever just happened, you should be proud.

Moving beyond the banh mi, Wall's signature burger with five-spice bacon and Szechuan relish joins the city's best, the trio of hot dogs includes a very functional marriage of kimchi and a Kobe beef frankfurter, and the beef noodle soup is impossibly rich and savory. Not to give the impression that non-meat eaters should stick to the drink menu—the coconut milk-based roasted carrot soup with Thai basil salsa verde is an all-diet pleaser, the red curry tofu meets all dietary needs (GF *and* V), and there's even an orange sesame Soy Curl banh mi.

On the bar end of things, there are four rotating taps and serious signature cocktails—try the Paloma with housemade jalapeño syrup or Thai tea syrup-spiked Stay Classy, Bangkok. Which is also good advice for the girl in the corner, spattered with miso bacon gravy and nearly buried under a mound of napkins.

MUST EATS

Green papaya salad, roast duck banh mi, Szechuan burger, kimchi dog, curried coconut ramen

SIDE DISH

If you're coveting the 50 taps and buzzy patio scene directly across the street at Apex beer bar, it's okay to defect—Apex has a relaxed BYOEats policy and welcomes outside food, even giant banh mi with 100-napkin entourages.

DETAILS

+ No reservations
+ Street parking is free and can be difficult to find

HOURS

TUE–SUN. . . . 11:30am-12am

1235 SE DIVISION STREET
503.230.8340 • *doubledragonpdx.com*

\$\$\$\$ *Credit Cards Accepted*

DOVE VIVI

PIZZA *in* KERNS

Sandwiched between a dry cleaners and a mini-mart in a tiny Northeast Portland strip mall, Dove Vivi is easy to miss—the first time around, there's a good chance you'll drive right by, distracted by neighboring Pambiche's amazing technicolor dreamfacade. So, as you approach the intersection of Restaurant Row and NE Glisan, be sure to keep your eyes peeled for the giant heart billboard, then zero in on the darling criss-crossed wooden hearts dangling from the roof, and finally, follow the scent of freshly-baked cornmeal crust pizza wafting into the parking lot—it won't take long to discover that this seemingly mundane strip mall conceals something quite remarkable.

Inside, the busy little pizzeria is modestly adorned with simple wood bench seating and an eclectic array of vintage prints, plus a roomy nook complete with thoughtfully-stocked magazine rack, where those waiting for a table or takeout can socialize, or just sit and scope out the cold case, which is filled with Mason jars of pickled vegetables and bowls of kale and beets destined for one of Dove Vivi's so-fresh-they-should-be-slapped salads, like the shredded kale and ricotta salata tossed with zingy lemon shallot dressing, a virtuous pizza dinner prelude.

Dove Vivi seems perpetually packed, unsurprising considering there's nothing else like it around—chefs/owners Gavin Blackstock and Delane Hamik bake their deep-dish cornmeal crust pies in cast iron pans, creating hearty, richly-flavored pizzas like the smoked mozzarella, fresh corn and sausage-topped *Corn*, pleasingly cheesy *Quatro Fromaggio*, and *Potato Pancetta*—paper thin slices of tender potato over mozzarella with pancetta and rosemary. The wine list is a superb value, and you can choose from three draft beers or a couple dozen bottled. Curb appeal or no, Dove Vivi is strip mall dining at its finest.

MUST EATS

Kale salad, iceberg wedge salad, arugula and pickled tomato pizza, corn and smoked mozzarella pizza, homemade zuccotto

SIDE DISH

One of Dove Vivi's many positive attributes is the ability to order your pizza three ways—whole, half, or slice, so even if you're friendless with a very small stomach and no way of preserving leftovers, you can still experience the Dove Vivi joy. You can also get parbaked pizzas to go and cook them at home.

DETAILS

+ No reservations
+ There's a small parking lot in front, and street parking is free and generally easy to find

HOURS

DAILY.............4-10pm

. . . .

2727 NE GLISAN STREET

503.239.4444 + *dovevivipizza.com*

. . . .

**$$**$$ *Credit Cards Accepted*

FIREHOUSE

ITALIAN *in* WOODLAWN

This North Portland restaurant is so comfortable that when I dine here I almost feel like I'm eating at a good neighbor's house—a neighbor who is a trained chef and enviably-skilled do-it-yourselfer and whose *Sunset Magazine*-worthy garden and patio puts my tiny backyard patch of moss-drowned brick and weed-choked "lawn" to shame. A neighbor like chef Matthew Busetto. Busetto—along with his wife Elizabeth, a naturopathic physician whose practice occupies the second floor of the building—bought and lovingly restored and refurbished the Woodlawn neighborhood's historic Firehouse 29 to its former glory in 2007, installing a wood-fired oven and rotisserie, uncovering the original brick walls and wide wooden beams, building the bar and furniture from reclaimed wood, laying an elegant stone patio, and planting the lush garden that surrounds the building. As a result, Firehouse has ambiance in spades, the rustic-chic aesthetics melding seamlessly with a friendly, laid-back atmosphere that makes it ideal for all occasions, be it a quiet midweek meal with your sweetheart or boisterous Saturday night family supper.

The menu showcases the garden's bounty in simple, satisfying dishes like fried cauliflower with lemon crème fraîche, meatballs with tomato and basil-braised green beans, thyme-rubbed rotisserie chicken alongside a salad of garden lettuces, and wood-fired Neapolitan-style pizzas topped with housemade meats, fresh mozzarella, and seasonal vegetables, all of which pairs quite nicely with a bottle of wine from the affordable, predominantly Italian wine list. Yes, Firehouse is the kind of neighbor everyone wants to be friends with. Now, if only they had a pool.

MUST EATS

Fried cauliflower, iron-skillet mussels, fennel sausage pizza, meatballs, rotisserie chicken

SIDE DISH

Firehouse pastry chef Gretchen Glatte's sweet and savory treats can be enjoyed all day long at Woodlawn Coffee and Pastry, a beautiful neighborhood coffeehouse and dessert catering kitchen across the street from the restaurant. Relax with Stumptown coffee, fresh-baked pastries, meatloaf sandwiches, polenta cake with molasses-cured pork belly, and homemade pie. Or, place a special order for a sherry olive oil cake or pumpkin chiffon pie.

DETAILS

+ Reservations accepted via phone or *opentable.com*
+ Street parking is free and easy to find

HOURS

MON-THU 5-9pm
FRI-SAT 5-9:30pm
SUN 5-8pm

. . . .

711 NE DEKUM STREET

503.954.1702 + *firehousepdx.com*

. . . .

**$$$**$ *Credit Cards Accepted*

GRÜNER

ALPINE *in* **DOWNTOWN**

During my last trip to Europe, I spent a fair amount of time in the Alpine region and frankly, I don't remember most of the places I ate at being nearly as posh as Grüner, Portland's principal purveyor of "cozy Alpine cuisine." Not that I'm complaining, I like a little posh in my life as much as the next girl, and sometimes luxurious leather banquettes and flickering olive-oil fed votives and juniper-cured wild salmon with cucumber radish salad are far preferable to a sauerkraut overdose and stifling cave-like pubs that reek of stale spilt lager.

Chef/owner Chris Israel's menu is a challenge for any serious diner, Alpine cuisine savvy or not, because if you're anything like me, you'll want to order everything. How do you choose between ricotta and Swiss chard dumplings, double-cut pork chops with red-wine poached wild plums, grilled golden trout swimming in horseradish cream, and spicy duck sausage stuffed quail? I agree, you don't. You'll have to round up a group of friends, take over the communal table occupying the back of the restaurant, and order everything to share.

You won't encounter the scent of stale spilt beer in this sleek little restaurant—the signature cocktails mixed and muddled in the birch-tree accented adjoining bar are tasty and pack a Teutonic wallop, teetotalers can refresh with a zesty spiced ginger house soda, and wine lovers will enjoy deciphering the unusual, and sometimes hard to pronounce wine list. Shall we share a bottle of Blaufränkisch with our sauerbraten, liebchen?

MUST EATS

Raclette croquettes, Grüner salad, coq au Riesling, quark spätzle with Black Forest ham, rhubarb cake with rhubarb ice cream

SIDE DISH

Grüner's semi-private Stammtisch (aka the "regulars'" table), which seats up to 12, is the ideal setting for an elegant family supper, German class get-together, or Crying Over Spilt Lager Club meetup.

DETAILS

- Reservations accepted via phone or *opentable.com*
- Street parking is metered and can be difficult to find

HOURS

MON-FRI ... 11:30am-2pm
MON-THU 5-9:30pm
FRI-SAT 5-10:30pm
Happy Hour
MON-FRI 4:30-6pm

. . . .

527 SW 12TH AVENUE
503.241.7163 • *grunerpdx.com*

. . . .

**$$$**$ *Credit Cards Accepted*

HA VL

VIETNAMESE *in* POWELLHURST-GILBERT

There are very few things that can get me up early on a Saturday—fresh doughnuts, road trips to cheese festivals, the need to beat a serious brunch line, and the fear of Ha VL soup shortages.

You see, every day Ha VL's charming chef/owner Ha "Christina" Luu makes a certain amount of the soup of the day and when that soup is gone, with a gleam in her eye and sorrowful amusement in her voice, Luu might tell you something like, "No more soup. Lucky for me, not lucky for you."* Since I like to get lucky, so to speak, with Saturday's soup of the day—the Bun Bo Hue, a rich spicy noodle soup with strips of tenderloin beef, spongy pork balls, and lemongrass—I set my early alarm and sleep fitfully, dreaming of vanishing pork balls and empty bowls.

Finding Ha VL the first time can be a challenge; it's secreted away in the north corner of tiny Wing Ming Square mall at SE 82nd and SE Clinton, just up the way from the legendary Fubonn Market. While it doesn't look like much from the outside, the little soup shop is as warm and charming as can be, with avocado green walls, lovingly arranged bric-a-brac, a curiously ample supply of colored straws, and an array of colorful canned refreshments, everything from pop to Yeo's and Foco fruit juices to Capri Suns. Luu, along with co-owner William Vuong, keeps a careful eye on her hungry patrons as she stirs and scoops her gorgeous soups and assembles crispy banh mi sandwiches, her tiny kitchen surrounded by hanging crystals and wind chimes—harbringers of, yes, luck.

Sadly, a true story.

MUST EATS

Spicy beef noodle soup, shrimp cake noodle soup, shredded noodle soup, crabflake noodle soup, sardine banh mi

SIDE DISH

Ha VL is best known for superb soups, but also offers a dozen or so banh mi, all of which can be ordered to go if you need a $3 lunch on the run.

DETAILS	HOURS
• No reservations	WED-MON 8am-4pm
• There is a small free parking lot out front	

2738 SE 82ND AVENUE • 503.772.0103

$$$$ *Credit Cards Accepted*

JADE TEAHOUSE
& PATISSERIE

VIETNAMESE *in* SELLWOOD

Jade is not the hushed, dim, contemplative nest of tranquility that might come to mind when one thinks "teahouse." Blessed with copious amounts of natural lighting, an airy treehouse-like feel, and a tidy bamboo-fringed patio, it's an ever-popular destination for all manner of local folk—toned Lycra short pants-wearing patrons of nearby Sellwood Yoga studio having heart-to-hearts over prawn and pork-stuffed lettuce rolls, Eastmoreland ladies who lunch taking a grilled tofu salad minibreak from their routine country club meetups, and herbal-tea sipping moms/dads sharing platefuls of stir-fried rice noodles with towheaded pixies in pink cowboys boots whose swinging feet don't quite reach the warm wood floors.

Flanked by the funky antique stores, coffee shops, boutiques and food carts that shape this charming stretch of SE 13th Avenue, Jade Teahouse serves Vietnamese fare with a French twist to a long, squiggly line of fans that often stretches all the way to the door a few minutes after opening. In harmony with the small-town feel of the neighborhood, Jade's a family affair—owner April Eklund convinced her mother Lucy to come out of retirement to fill the pastry case with baked bliss, and her father Mark can be spotted behind the register, congenially chatting with regulars, patiently discussing the merits of chicken verses shrimp with first-timers, and encouraging everyone to indulge in something sweet—be it a coconut cupcake with lemon hibiscus sauce, sesame ball, or white chocolate macaron with sea salt. True to its name, Jade stocks nearly 80 types of Foxfire, Jasmine Pearl, and custom-blended teas on revolving shelves that stretch to the ceiling, so you'll have no trouble finding a loose leaf soul mate for your brick of bright green Vietnamese Wedding Cake, a dessert so popular, each patron is limited to only two pieces.

MUST EATS

Grilled eggplant with sweet and sour basil sauce, BBQ pork hum bao, green papaya and shrimp salad, yellow curry, Vietnamese wedding cake (because it's green, and green cake is fun)

SIDE DISH

Jade Teahouse doesn't have table service; you order at the register and find your own seat. If it's busy (likely), I suggest assigning an operative to seek and secure a table while you order, or vice versa.

DETAILS	HOURS
• No reservations	MON-SAT...... 11am-9pm
• Street parking is free and generally easy to find	

. . . .

7912 SE 13TH AVENUE
503.477.8985 • *jadeportland.com*

. . . .

**$$**$$ *Credit Cards Accepted*

JAMES JOHN CAFÉ

NEW AMERICAN *in* ST. JOHNS

Once upon a time, I was a Portland Public Schools substitute teacher, and occasionally I'd be assigned to James John Elementary. After a long morning in the classroom, I'd cut across the playground and head into downtown St. Johns for lunch. Over time, I developed a real soft spot for this plucky Portland annex, because while it isn't always much to look at, it's got heart.

Along the main street, busy Tienda and Taqueria Santa Cruz sells delightfully garish piñatas and tasty dollar tacos, old-timey Blue Moon camera shop makes sure lovingly-restored typewriters go to good homes, Barrique Barrel bottle shop and The Olive & Vine specialty market keep everyone well-watered and fed, the proud volunteer-run farmers' market brightens the plaza come summer, and James John Café nurtures the neighborhood with from-scratch pastries, hearty sandwiches, roasted vegetable bread pudding, smoked trout hash, biscuits 'n gravy, cassoulet, excellent coffee, and a full bar.

The unassuming, black-awning sheltered storefront opens up into a spacious, peaceful café with soaring pressed-tin ceilings, well-worn sofas framing a coffee table strewn with NYT sections, and a vintage bar lined with locals sipping Stumptown coffee, fresh-squeezed lemonade, and PBR. The décor is sparse but interesting—deer heads hang on the walls above muted still lifes of fruit, and an antlered rabbit with a saucy expression is mounted above the doorway to the kitchen. Now and then, chefs/owners Aaron Solley and Suzanne Bozarth (former bar manager at Paley's Place) host fun events like pig roasts, crawfish boils, and communal dinners with seasonal menus that might include mushroom consommé, pickled shrimp salad, braised short ribs with horseradish potatoes, and espresso pot de crème. Pushing back from the table afterwards, you'll seriously consider relocating to St. Johns, for the food *and* the piñatas.

MUST EATS

Biscuits with chocolate gravy, breakfast sandwich, corned beef hash, cassoulet, chicken salad sandwich

SIDE DISH

If you'd like to get the email invites to James John Café's family-style suppers and neighborhood events, let Suzanne and Aaron know at *jamesjohncafe@gmail.com*.

DETAILS

- Reservations accepted for suppers via phone or email
- Street parking is free and generally easy to find

HOURS

TUE-SUN 9am-2pm

. . . .

8527 N LOMBARD STREET
503.285.4930 ◆ *jamesjohncafe.com*

. . . .

**$$**$$ *Credit Cards Accepted*

KEN'S ARTISAN BAKERY

BAKERY *in the* ALPHABET DISTRICT

I spend a lot of time fantasizing about what it would be like to live in Paris, but when I claim a seat at Ken's big wooden farmhouse table, Stumptown café au lait and the Sunday *New York Times* in hand, and tear a smoldering pain du chocolat from limb to limb, watching the warm chocolate ooze out from between the buttery golden layers of pastry, I'm thinking there's no place like Portland. While perusing the travel section, I tuck into a lemon meringue tartlet, gently plucking off each golden meringue tip before biting through the thin, crisp buttery crust into the silky sweet-tart lemon cream. On my way out, I order a half dozen dusty pink rosewater macarons for my Ken's-besotted neighbor, a slice of hazelnut poundcake for Mom, a loaf of walnut bread for dinner, and a piece of opera cake to pleadingly offer up to the gods of outrageously discounted PDX-CDG airfare.

If you're a west-side vampire unable to cross the briskly-flowing waters of the Willamette, or are in some other way prevented from making the trek to SE 28th Avenue for Ken's Artisan Pizza, get the next best thing—every Monday evening starting at 5:30pm, the bakery hosts its wildly popular Monday Night Pizza, the success of which was the impetus for the opening of

100 Best Places to Stuff Your faces

A MOUTHWATERING CHECKLIST OF
THE MOST DELICIOUS, DELIGHTFUL
AND UNIQUE DINING EXPERIENCES
IN PORTLAND, OREGON

2ND EDITION
with 35 new places...

- ☐ Accanto
- ☐ Alma Chocolate
- ☐ Andina
- ☐ Apizza Scholls
- ☐ Ataula
- ☐ Ava Gene's
- ☐ Aviary
- ☐ Bamboo Sushi
- ☐ Bar Avignon
- ☐ Beast
- ☐ Biwa
- ☐ Bluehour
- ☐ Blueplate
- ☐ Boke Bowl
- ☐ Bollywood Theater
- ☐ Broder
- ☐ Bunk Sandwiches
- ☐ Cacao

Keep eating! The list continues on the back of this bookmark...

* * * * * * * * * * * * *

- ☐ Candy Babel
- ☐ Canteen
- ☐ Cartopia
- ☐ Castagna
- ☐ Cheese Bar
- ☐ Chef Naoko Bento Café
- ☐ Clarklewis
- ☐ Clyde Common
- ☐ The Country Cat
- ☐ Cyril's
- ☐ Dar Salam
- ☐ Din Din
- ☐ DOC
- ☐ Double Dragon
- ☐ Dove Vivi
- ☐ Firehouse
- ☐ Grüner
- ☐ Ha VL
- ☐ Jade Teahouse & Patisserie
- ☐ James John Café
- ☐ Ken's Artisan Bakery
- ☐ Ken's Artisan Pizza
- ☐ Lardo
- ☐ Laurelhurst Market
- ☐ Lauretta Jean's
- ☐ Le Pigeon
- ☐ Levant
- ☐ Little Bird
- ☐ Little T American Baker
- ☐ Lovely's Fifty-Fifty
- ☐ Maurice
- ☐ Meat Cheese Bread
- ☐ Mississippi Marketplace
- ☐ Natural Selection
- ☐ Ned Ludd
- ☐ Noisette
- ☐ Nong's Khao Man Gai
- ☐ Nostrana
- ☐ Nuestra Cocina
- ☐ Nuvrei
- ☐ The Ocean

- ☐ Old Salt Marketplace
- ☐ Olympic Provisions
- ☐ Ox
- ☐ PaaDee
- ☐ Pacific Pie Company
- ☐ Paley's Place
- ☐ Park Kitchen
- ☐ PDX671
- ☐ Pearl Bakery
- ☐ Piazza Italia
- ☐ Pine State Biscuits
- ☐ Pip's Original
- ☐ Pix Patisserie/Bar Vivant
- ☐ Pod 28
- ☐ Podnah's Pit BBQ
- ☐ Pok Pok
- ☐ Por Qué No
- ☐ Portland Farmers' Market
- ☐ Ración
- ☐ Roe/Block + Tackle
- ☐ Ruby Jewel
- ☐ Saint Cupcake
- ☐ Salt & Straw
- ☐ Sauvage
- ☐ Screen Door
- ☐ Simpatica Dining Hall
- ☐ Smallwares
- ☐ St. Jack
- ☐ The Sugar Cube
- ☐ Sweedeedee
- ☐ Tabor Bread
- ☐ Tanuki
- ☐ Tasty n Sons
- ☐ Teote
- ☐ Toro Bravo
- ☐ Two Tarts Bakery
- ☐ Viking Soul Food
- ☐ Waffle Window
- ☐ Wildwood
- ☐ Woodsman Tavern
- ☐ Xico

* * * by Jen Stevenson   wordcake.com * * *

the eastside pizzeria. Tucked into a small window table with a Caesar salad, the spicy soppressata pizza, and a glass of very good wine, I can't help but wonder—even if I had the chance to move to Paris, how could I *ever* leave Ken's?!

MUST EATS

Chocolate croissant, pear ginger upside down cake, jambon and Asiago sandwich, fresh grapefruit tart, raisin pecan bread

SIDE DISH

Just over the Morrison Bridge, you'll find baker/owner Ken Forkish's third culinary act, a bakery-tavern hybrid dubbed Trifecta (*726 SE 6th Ave.*). Described as both his atelier and a "mishmash [of] the DNA of Chez Panisse's cafe, Animal, and Joe Beef," Trifecta spotlights Ken's famous breads and pastries, plus sophisticated pub grub, gorgeous desserts, craft cocktails, and very good bottles of wine, many courtesy of Ken's own cellar.

DETAILS	HOURS	
• No reservations	MON-SAT	7am-6pm
• Street parking is free and difficult to find, but you can park in neighboring Bastas' parking lot until 5pm	SUN	8am-5pm
	Pizza Night	
	MON	5:30-9:30pm

. . . .

338 NW 21ST AVENUE

503.248.2202 • *kensartisan.com*

. . . .

**$$**$$ *Credit Cards Accepted*

KEN'S ARTISAN PIZZA

PIZZA *in* KERNS

No matter how often I stroll 28th Avenue's Restaurant Row around dinnertime, every time I see the familiar cluster of folks standing on the corner of SE 28th and Pine, I'm concerned/perplexed/intrigued. And every time, when I nosily investigate, there's no great spectacle or box of kittens to be found, I'm just witness yet again to the ever-present lineup of Ken's Artisan Pizza enthusiasts patiently waiting their turn for these seemingly addictive wood-fired pies.

Owner Ken Forkish's small but mighty Artisan Empire expanded in 2006 to include this high-energy Southeast pizzeria where, even seven years later, when one could arguably say the novelty has worn off, it's still nearly impossible to walk in and sit down expeditiously. The dining room can feel compact at full tide—the tables are so close together you'll practically eat with your elbows in someone else's Margherita, but claustrophobia is averted thanks to huge wraparound windows that create an airy feeling and let the evening breeze in on warm summer nights.

Ken's crown jewel is the custom-built pizza oven that bakes with such intensity that chef/co-founder Alan Maniscalco's pies are cooked in a scant two minutes, the thin crust rendered perfectly chewy and blistered, the seasonal toppings barely disturbed. Start your meal with a Caesar, house-smoked trout salad, or roasted vegetable plate, then move on to the star attraction—the Soppressata is my pizza soul mate, but there are a dozen or so to choose from.

Ken's has four beers on tap and more than 100 excellent wines, and a handful of uncomplicated desserts that let you linger just a few moments longer before you reluctantly relinquish your table to the next group, ruefully recognizing the familiar gleam of pizza lust shining in their eyes.

MUST EATS

Caesar, roasted vegetable plate, oven-roasted calamari, soppressata pizza, margherita pizza

SIDE DISH

If you want takeout pizza from Ken's, you'll have to put away your phone and work for it—the kitchen accepts *walk-in* to-go orders only, Monday through Thursday.

DETAILS

- No reservations
- Street parking is free and generally easy to find

HOURS

MON-SAT.........5-10pm

SUN 4-9pm

. . . .

304 SE 28TH AVENUE

503.517.9951 • kensartisan.com

. . . .

**$$$**$ *Credit Cards Accepted*

LARDO

SANDWICHES *in* HOSFORD-ABERNETHY/DOWNTOWN

It's really best if you leave all gustatory inhibitions at the doors of these crazy-busy sandwich shops—after all, when the first thing you spy with your pork-loving eye upon walking into a restaurant is a huge lit-up sign admonishing you to PIG OUT, I think we both know that as far as your diet diary is concerned, what happens in Lardo stays in Lardo.

But if you're going to stray from the caloric straight and narrow, you might as well do it right, and there are few more enjoyable failings than chef Rick Gencarelli's pork belly sandwich—glistening, hot fat streaked slabs of this most hallowed Portland mainstay laid to rest on a pillow-soft, golden-crusted Fleur de Lis Bakery brioche bun, or the bacon-topped cold fried chicken sandwich slathered in buttermilk blue cheese dressing, or the epic Double Burger, or the pork scraps and marinated -peppers littered "dirty fries," or the three microbrews/grapefruit margaritas you wash it all down with. You sinner, you.

While the menu does delve deep into meat territory, herbivores needn't feel excluded—sit right alongside your favorite pork meatball banh mi worshipper with a hearty eggplant and fennel sandwich and light and lemony kale Caesar, or a simple, perfect dish of roasted zucchini tossed with lemon, cracked black pepper and fresh mint. So, if it's Meatless Monday or you *are* for some strange reason on a diet, in the immortal words of *Caddyshack*'s Carl Spackler, you got that goin' for you, which is nice.

MUST EATS

Crispy pig ear salad, dirty fries, pork belly sandwich, smoked coppa Cubano, double burger

SIDE DISH

While Lardo's menu may be bereft of sugary swan songs, fear not—sweets await just beyond the front doors of each location. On the eastside, Hungry Heart Cupcakes' truck is so close you can practically place an order from your patio table, and the downtown Lardo is right across the street from Ruby Jewel's West End scoop shop, and just around the corner from the city's most revered chocolate church, Cacao.

DETAILS

+ No reservations
+ Street parking is free and generally easy to find at SE, metered and difficult to find at the downtown location

HOURS

SE Location

SUN-THU	11am-11pm
FRI-SAT	11am-12am

SW Location

DAILY	11am-10pm

. . . .

1212 SE HAWTHORNE BLVD ✦ 503.234.7786
1205 SW WASHINGTON ST. ✦ 503.241.2490
lardopdx.com

. . . .

**$$**$$ *Credit Cards Accepted*

LAURELHURST MARKET

"STEAKHOUSE" *in* KERNS

A food lover's life is marked by food phases, periods of time during which we obsessively embrace one culinary fetish or another for often unknown reasons. In my case, there's been the boxed mashed potato phase (I know, embarrassing), homemade popsicles phase, juicing phase, South Beach phase (also embarrassing), sweetbreads phase, and gluten-free phase. Back in college, there was the F. McLintock's phase, a dalliance with a wildly-popular Pismo Beach steakhouse not far from my alma mater, Cal Poly San Luis Obispo. They served massive T-bones and tri-tip, filled water glasses with their back turned without spilling a drop, and on your birthday they'd sing to you, snap a Polaroid of your obliging grimace and put it in a nice card for your scrapbook.

Laurelhurst Market doesn't take a Polaroid on my birthday and so far I've only experienced rudimentary water pouring, but the devout attention they pay to meat dredges up welcome memories of my unabashed-carnivorism phase. Unlike a stereo-typical steakhouse, however, Laurelhurst Market sidesteps the aw-shucks aesthetics and routine cuisine in favor of chef Dave Kreifel's sophisticated, seasonally-influenced menu, which is brawny (steak tartare, steak frites, ribeye with blue cheese butter, double-cut pork chop, 12-hour-smoked brisket) but sensitive (grilled eggplant caponata, heirloom melon and Basque pepper salad, figs with prosciutto, farro and lobster mushrooms). The modern concrete and wood dining room is as smooth and classy as the fine single malt scotches served in the stylish little indoor/outdoor bar, making Laurelhurst a quintessential neighborhood brasserie, butcher shop, sandwich joint, and first-rate bar in one pretty package, with an equally diverse clientele and reputation that can prompt lengthy waits. It could easily become your next, and most enduring, food phase.

MUST EATS

Wedge salad, Baird peaches with house ham, steak tartare, marrow bones, Piedmontese teres major

SIDE DISH

Laurelhurst Market is owned by the same trio of meat-loving guys behind Simpatica Dining Hall and the former Viande Meats & Sausage, and their expertise shows in the full-service butcher shop adjoining the restaurant. The case is brimming with all-natural, hormone-free and antibiotic-free meats, hand-stuffed sausages, smoked ham, pâtés, lardo and duck confit. A serious sandwich list hangs on the wall, and on Tuesdays only, fried chicken is sold by the pound starting at 11am.

DETAILS	HOURS
• Reservations accepted via phone and website	*Restaurant* DAILY.............5-10pm
• Private free lot in front and street parking is free and generally easy to find	*Butcher Shop* DAILY..........10am-10pm

. . . .

3155 E BURNSIDE STREET

503.206.3097 *(restaurant)* • 503.206.3099 *(butcher shop)*

laurelhurstmarket.com

. . . .

\$\$\$\$ *Credit Cards Accepted*

LAURETTA JEAN'S

PIE *in* RICHMOND

Occasionally, people ask me how I became so interested in food and I pause, wondering which story I should tell, a florid, heartwarming tale of cooking family recipes with my Italian mother, or the truth, which is that my Italian mother is more of an "experimental" cook and that one time one of her "experimental" batches of oatmeal carob chip brown rice syrup cookies even made one of our goats sick. (We used to feed the goats all our kitchen scraps, poor souls.) But I do have one lovely childhood baking memory that I cling dearly to, that of Mom's inexplicably delicious tarts—rounds of flaky pie dough mounded with raspberry jam, then folded over and crimped to make perfect half-moon shaped tarts, which we'd eat hot from the oven, burning our fingers, tongues, and the goats' tongues in the process. (Just kidding, *those* tarts never made it to the goat field.)

I get fond flashbacks to those happy tart times the moment I walk into this exquisitely homey Division Street pie shop, a vision of white wainscoting, mint green walls trimmed in gold, and a glass pastry case stuffed with all manner of crust and crumb magnificence—chocolate chess pies, raspberry currant pies, peach cake, apricot almond scones and chocolate chip cookies. Savory is given its due, via ham and cheese hand pies, zucchini bread, and asparagus and roasted spring onion quiche, and during the relaxed weekend brunch, hearty dishes like the lox galette, ratatouille on garlic toast, and smoked ham Benedict on a house biscuit. Speaking of which, there may not be a better biscuit to be found, and it can be had with strawberry jam, warmed and served with soup on a rainy afternoon, or simply eaten plain straight from the pastry stand. When you're done, get a few to go for my mom's goats—they could likely use a treat.

MUST EATS

Apple brandy blackberry pie, chocolate cream pie, biscuit with homemade strawberry jam, quiche, smoked ham Benedict

SIDE DISH

Can't make it to the Southeast shop? Lauretta Jean's has a teeny-tiny downtown annex (*600 SW Pine St.; 503.224.9236*) and a pieriffic booth at the PSU Farmers' Market on Saturdays.

DETAILS	HOURS	
• No reservations	MON-FRI	9am-10pm
• Street parking is free and generally easy to find	SAT	8am-10pm
	SUN	8am-5pm
	Brunch	
	SAT-SUN	8am-3pm

. . . .

3402 SE DIVISION STREET
503.235.3119 • *laurettajean.com*

. . . .

**$**$$$ *Credit Cards Accepted*

LE PIGEON

FRENCH *in* BUCKMAN

Unfortunately, my most tenacious recollection of Le Pigeon will forever be the time I was standing outside the big front window following a particularly pleasant dinner party and my "best friend" flipped my dress up, exposing my plump rump to the whole restaurant...but Le Pigeon's rich, hearty beef cheek (ha, ha) bourguignon and famous/infamous foie gras ice cream-stuffed profiteroles follow as close seconds.

This rustic little brick-walled bistro's menu is short, sweet, and a worthy challenge for both the fledgling and well-seasoned epicure. Chef/owner Gabe Rucker—a colorful local character who has been lauded in practically every food and culture publication there is—puts his unique stamp on classic French fare in an open kitchen the size of a (small) closet, pairing pig's foot with watermelon, rabbit terrine with eel and miso, and serving the eponymous pigeon anointed with foie gras and Riesling. And speaking of wine, Le Pigeon's list is always a pleasure, filled with delights both known and unusual, with prices to fit every pocketbook.

Le Pigeon is one of Portland's foremost communal dining experiences—if you reserve a seat at one of the three wooden tables, you'll be quite intimate with your neighbors, so bring your Altoids and best party stories. Or, if you prefer a front-row view of the kitchen action to hobnobbing with strangers, sit at the 10-seat first-come-first-served Chef's Counter, which puts you so close to the stove you can almost touch the flock of pigeons tattooed on Gabe's forearm as he sears scallops and plates rabbit haunches. In parting, I have but one piece of hard-earned advice—if you dine here with your favorite prankster, please wear boy shorts under your dress.

MUST EATS

Beef cheek bourguignon, sweetbreads, rabbit blanquette, Le Pigeon burger, foie gras profiteroles

SIDE DISH

Le Pigeon is known for inventive, upscale French-inspired fare, but the legendary house burger—a slab of juicy grilled local beef piled high with aged Tillamook white cheddar, grilled pickled onions and iceberg lettuce slaw on a Ken's Artisan Bakery ciabatta roll—gets its share of love, and rightfully so.

DETAILS

- Reservations accepted via phone or *opentable.com*
- Street parking is free and can be difficult to find

HOURS

DAILY 5-10pm

738 E BURNSIDE STREET

503.546.8796 • *lepigeon.com*

**$$$**$ *Credit Cards Accepted*

LEVANT

MIDDLE EASTERN *in* KERNS

Levant chef Scott Snyder counts one of his "French Arabesque" menu's culinary influences as the Ottoman Empire, but although I can't speak from experience, I'm going to assume that Levant is far more fun than the Ottoman Empire—it is military-skirmish free, has Moroccan mint ice cream sandwiches, and is warmer in the winter, thanks to the custom built six-foot-wide hearth with Tuscan-fireplace style grills embedded in the kitchen's brick wall, where Snyder and team slow cook coals-kissed dishes like grilled sardines with spicy roasted pepper salad, whole ears of corn dripping with preserved lime honey butter, and hearth-roasted lamb with caramelized quince and pomegranate lamb jus, accompanied by artful, off-the-grill small plates like pan-roasted lobster mushrooms with harissa and brown butter-drizzled red kuri squash soup.

Decorwise, the dining room strikes a becoming balance between modern and medieval, with tidy racks of firewood and wine, intricate tilework, dark concrete slab countertops, and a grand, tentacled metal chandelier clearly salvaged from a *Game of Thrones* set. Speaking of which, the only torture around these parts will be self-inflicted, in the form of skipping dessert, which

I highly *un*recommend, because the desserts are exquisite—the Turkish coffee custard-filled doughnuts, pear and date polenta crisp with burnt fig leaf ice cream, and ginger molasses cake with honey-whipped goat labneh will have you chanting 'Long live the Levant empire' long into the night, as you clink Fallen Jinns.

MUST EATS

Fried halloumi cheese, roasted carrots with zhoug, grilled sardine, hearth-roasted lamb, spicy ginger molasses cake

SIDE DISH

If you want to hold a secret summit with your fellow sultans, or maybe just your family and friends, reserve Levant's beautiful dark wood-paneled private dining room for parties of up to 8.

DETAILS

- Reservations accepted via phone or *opentable.com*
- Street parking is free and can be difficult to find

HOURS

TUE-SAT 5-10pm

. . . .

2448 E BURNSIDE STREET
503.954.2322 • *levantpdx.com*

. . . .

**$$**$$ *Credit Cards Accepted*

LITTLE BIRD

FRENCH *in* **DOWNTOWN**

You do not have to, in the now-immortal words of *Portlandia*, "put a bird on it" at this beautiful Paris-meets-Portland bistro, because someone already did. No, really. There are little birds everywhere. Little birds peeking out from various crevices and hidey-holes, little birds tucked into the wine rack, a dainty flock of *really* little snow-white ceramic birds flying across the bathroom wall, and gangs of glittery-eyed hoodlum crows skulking around outside the front door, casing the shiny pressed-tin ceiling. All right, so maybe that last one is an exaggeration, but I wouldn't be surprised. The ceiling *is* dazzling.

The brainchild of Le Pigeon restaurant's executive chef Gabriel Rucker and general manager Andy Fortgang, Little Bird's kitchen is helmed by longtime Le Pigeon sous chef Erik Van Kley, whose menu zeroes in on beloved, expertly-executed French bistro classics like steak frites, coq au vin, and marrow bones. Dessert is orchestrated by the talented Lauren Fortgang, who spins sweet fantasies like an alabaster cylinder of coconut cake flanked by a sublime passion fruit sorbet and milk chocolate hazelnut financier topped with candied kumquats.

Late hours, a central location, and flexible offerings make Little Bird an inviting downtown destination regardless of the hour (they're open until midnight) or your craving—stop in for a glass of wine and a charcuterie board or reserve a dark red leather half-booth for a relaxed supper.

You may prefer to hug the gleaming copper bar or see and be seen in the main dining room, but in my opinion the best seat in the house (provided you don't suffer from acrophobia) is the tiny corner table hugging the balcony. From this perch, you can observe the entire restaurant in motion, so not only can you people watch to your heart's content, but you'll also be the first to know if the crows decide to storm the ramparts and make off with the ceiling tiles.

MUST EATS

Macaroni gratin, coq au vin, duck leg and pork belly cassoulet, lamb ribs with chévre gougères, blackberry Crêpes Suzette

SIDE DISH

If you are fascinated by the inner workings of restaurant kitchens, you'll love watching Little Bird's—a wall of sidewalk-facing glass renders the kitchen ant farm-transparent, providing a fun sneak peek of the behind-the-scenes melee.

DETAILS	HOURS
• Reservations accepted via phone or *opentable.com*	MON-FRI . . 11:30am-12am
	SAT-SUN 5pm-12am
• Street parking is metered and can be difficult to find	

. . . .

219 SW 6TH AVENUE

503.688.5952 • *littlebirdbistro.com*

. . . .

**$$$**$ *Credit Cards Accepted*

LITTLE T AMERICAN BAKER

BAKERY in HOSFORD-ABERNETHY

I have a lot of guilty pleasures, mostly involving champagne, unguarded jars of dark chocolate sauce, and the Daily Mail Online's celebrity gossip section. I also like to look in other people's windows. I don't sneak around playing Peeping Tom or anything, but when I'm having a nice leisurely meander around town, I'm fascinated by the brief glimpse into random strangers' lives that a good peek in their front window offers. My favorite is a small Ladd's Addition bungalow where the bay window is almost entirely filled with a huge sleeping wolf-dog.

But when I gave Little T American Baker's spotless floor-to-ceiling window my cursory once-over, I nearly passed out from delighted shock and crippling envy. Because *their* window is filled with baker/owner Tim Helea's freshly-baked artisan bread, shelves and shelves of some of the most beautiful loaves you'll ever see—gently dimpled slabs of herb-dusted foccacia, orange-specked 7-grain carrot rolls, light golden baguettes, salt-crusted pretzel bread, and flour-dusted mounds of multigrain spelt. Venturing inside this minimalist-chic gluten haven, cautiously taking in the glossy concrete floors and shiny stainless steel countertops, I thought maybe I'd stumbled upon the Design Within Reach cafeteria, but the 50-pound sacks of flour along the back wall and the pastry case begged to differ—precisely-placed stacks of chewy molasses cookies speckled with coarse sugar crystals, fig-studded Danish, deep dark brownies, lemon-curd filled drop biscuits, ridiculously rich chocolate praline croissants, kouign amann and lemon tartlets all twinkled prettily in their glass-enclosed perch. Above, a chalkboard menu promised from-scratch soups and salads, and sandwiches crafted with house-cured Sockeye salmon, smoked trout salad, braised pork, and roasted vegetables, all made with that glorious bread. Okay, so maybe they don't have a sleeping wolf-dog in the window, but I'll take another ham and cheese on pretzel bread, three cupcakes, and a double chocolate croissant instead.

MUST EATS

Double chocolate croissant, Woodblock chocolate chip cookie, passion fruit cake, focaccia, whole wheat croissant egg sandwich

SIDE DISH

In fall 2013, Little T proudly announced the birth of their second bakery, affectionately dubbed "Tiny T." One of the diminutive tenants of West End's upscale Union Way alleyway micromall, it's open daily for downtowners' pastry pleasure (*1022 W Burnside St.; 503.894.8258*).

DETAILS	HOURS
• No reservations	MON-SAT....... 7am-5pm
• Street parking is free and generally easy to find	SUN 8am-2pm

2600 SE DIVISION STREET
503.238.3458 • *littletbaker.com*

$$$$ *Credit Cards Accepted*

LOVELY'S FIFTY-FIFTY

PIZZA *in* BOISE

In the name of research, I generally eat out every night, and if/
when I have kids, I don't see this changing—we're just going
to eat at Lovely's Fifty-Fifty every night. Oh *sure* Jen, you are
thinking, just you wait you smug childless eat-out-every-nighter,
when you have kids, the only thing you are going to be eating
every night is crow, and a lot of airborne puréed yams. But I have
thought this through, so hear me out!

After all, Lovely's Fifty-Fifty is perfectly equipped for family
dinners—they have big cozy booths, a laid-back vibe, and all
the food groups necessary for the entire family's well-rounded
diet: wood-fired pizza, unwaveringly seasonal salads and small
plates, creamy housemade ice cream, and very good wine. It's
good to be a kid here: your cheese pizza is only $7, you can slurp
homemade sodas, and nobody gives you a second glance when
you gleefully race the length of the restaurant, drenched in pizza
sauce and melted huckleberry buttermilk ice cream, squealing
something about macaroni flowers, while your parents dazedly
sip wine and nibble an heirloom tomato salad.

Lovely's Fifty-Fifty owners (and sisters) Sarah and Jane
Minnick have carved out this sweet, homey little nook along
hip North Mississippi Avenue, creating a space that walks the
line between modern and vintage, with high ceilings, massive
wood beams, a huge roll-up glass garage door, and an eclectic
collection of precisely-hung vintage prints lining the softly hued

walls. Lest I've overemphasized the family-friendliness, rest assured that Lovely's is a suppertime haven for the child-free and child-endowed alike, making for a lively neighborhood melting pot of top-notch vittles and people-watching. So...I'll see you there Tuesday through Sunday? Lovely's Fifty-Fifty is closed on Mondays, so that's when the kids will go to Grandma's (mark your calendar, Mom)!

MUST EATS

Roasted padron peppers, oven roasted green beans, Bellwether ricotta with gremolata pizza, spinach with fromage blanc, pounded garlic and bacon pizza, salted caramel ice cream

SIDE DISH

If you want to eat Lovely's Fifty-Fifty every night (except Monday) in the comfort of your home, they will happily take your to-go order—just call it in and pick it up. Or, if you're ear-deep in puréed yams, hire a TaskRabbit to pick it up.

DETAILS	HOURS
• Reservations accepted for parties of six or more	TUE-SUN 5-10pm
• Street parking is free and generally easy to find	

. . . .

4039 N MISSISSIPPI AVENUE
503.281.4060 • lovelysfiftyfifty.com

. . . .

**$$**$$ *Credit Cards Accepted*

MAURICE

PASTRY LUNCHEONETTE *in* **DOWNTOWN**

In the grand scheme of things, Portlanders have it *very* good. Oh sure, we have problems like everyone else—because of the 856-inch average yearly rainfall*, many of us suffer from terrible WSS (wet sock syndrome), due to all the ace coffee roasters, we are often dangerously overcaffeinated, and thanks to the abundance of first-rate restaurants, most residents are perpetually wearing our skinny jeans one size too small. Aside from these minor issues, however, we've been under the impression that we want for nothing. But sometimes, you don't know what you're missing until it hits you in the tongue with a rhubarb vacherin, and as it turns out, all these years, none of us had any idea that there was a huge gaping void in our culinary lives—a pastry luncheonette. (Cue angels singing and Moscato d'Asti corks popping.)

Fortunately, posh restaurant pastry chef turned pastry luncheonette proprietress, Kristen Murray, has stepped in to save us all from a existence bereft of mango tarte tatin and cocoa puff palmiers by opening this nectarous new concept in a sweet space tucked down a pleasantly mellow tree-lined street in downtown's happening West End neighborhood. Armed with a pastry background and aesthetic so impressive that entire shelves of sugar bags bow and curtsy in unison as she glides down the grocery store dry goods aisle, Kristen conjures up stunning sweet somethings like duck egg flan with chocolate consommé, geranium-scented pain perdu, and black pepper cheesecake with rhubarb-apple confiture and celery leaf gelée, served alongside craft cocktails and fine wines, on the heels of Maurice's daytime "luncheonette" menu. But as wondrous as this all is, with mo' honey comes mo' problems, problems like skinny jeans that are now *two* sizes too small.

By my socks' best estimate

MUST EATS

Rhubarb vacherin, caramel mousse trifles with chocolate banana jam, black pepper cheesecake, cocoa puff palmier, mini macarons

SIDE DISH

Ensure regular sugar fixes delivered right into your waiting arms by joining Maurice's bi-monthly Community Supported Pastry Parcel program, which might include miniature macarons and kumquat marmalade one shipment, sultana hazelnut truffles and burnt sugar and chocolate cajeta the next.

DETAILS

- No reservations
- Street parking is metered and can be difficult to find

HOURS

DAILY......... 10am-10pm

. . . .

921 SW OAK STREET

503.224.9921 • *mauricepdx.com*

. . . .

**$$**$$ *Credit Cards Accepted*

MEAT CHEESE BREAD

SANDWICHES *in* BUCKMAN

Most of us have had past love interests who were scared off by one or another of the more threatening "three little words" expressions, such as: I Love You, Maybe I'm Pregnant, Your Mother's Hot, I'm a Vegan, I'm a Carnivore, etc. But there's one three-word phrase that won't make your skittish beau break a cold sweat when you whisper it in his/her ear—Meat Cheese Bread. In fact, he/she will probably up and declare their undying affection right then and there. With good reason too, because chef/owner John Stewart's funky Southeast sandwich shop has perfected a trinity that's right up there with Air Water Food, and since it's open from 7am to 8pm, you can eat its three-element divinity for Breakfast Lunch Dinner.

Start the day with the Steak and Egg, a real meal of a breakfast sandwich stacked with sliced flank steak, blue cheese, and a fried egg, or the much-loved breakfast burrito—a flour tortilla stuffed with scrambled eggs, hash browns, green chile salsa, and cheddar (meat optional—get the ham). For lunch, try the twist-on-a-classic B.L.B.—Nueske's smoked bacon, lettuce, and roasted heirloom beets piled on housemade sourdough, or the warm flank steak, blue cheese mayo and pickled onions-packed Park Kitchen, named after Stewart's former employer and long-revered Portland culinary mainstay.

Even though man/woman can technically live by meat cheese bread alone, the shop ladles up first-rate soups and stews, robust salads (most sandwiches can be converted into a salad too), and one of my favorite chocolate fleur de sel cookies ever, in addition to locally-made Ruby Jewel ice cream sandwiches and Xocolatl de David confections. You know, just writing this, I think I've Fallen In Love with Meat Cheese Bread all over again.

MUST EATS

Flank steak and fried egg breakfast sandwich, breakfast burrito with ham, Park Kitchen sandwich, grilled green bean and soft boiled egg sandwich, crème fraiche brownie

SIDE DISH

If you were reading and rereading the words Meat Cheese Bread with the nagging feeling that something was missing, followed by the realization that what's missing is Beer, you're in luck—Stewart opened a handsome beer bar next door to his sandwich shop, with a dozen taps and over 100 bottled beers. If you get hungry, order Meat Cheese Bread next door and they'll bring it to you at Beer. And just like that, your life is complete.

DETAILS	HOURS
• No reservations	DAILY.......... 7am-8pm
• Street parking is free and generally easy to find	

. . . .

1406 SE STARK STREET

503.234.1700 • *meatcheesebread.com*

. . . .

\$\$\$\$ *Credit Cards Accepted*

MISSISSIPPI MARKETPLACE

CART POD *in* BOISE

There are loads of perfectly good reasons to make a beeline for the corner of Mississippi and Skidmore. Perhaps you've always wanted to drink pilsner from a glass boot in a beautifully-renovated turn-of-the-century bierhouse. You can. Perhaps you need to launder a load of PBR-soaked hoodies. You can do that too. Or, maybe you need a luxury condo for you and your teacup pig, or historic former conservatory in which to host your nonprofit event. Check and check. Most critically of all, you may require a kimchi and bulgogi-beef topped Korean hot dog, bowl of piping hot ramen, or applewood-smoked ham, blackberry jam, mascarpone and basil brioche sandwich.

Once again, you're in luck, for this well-endowed corner of North Portland is home to one of the city's most beloved cart pods, Mississippi Marketplace—a tidy lineup of 10 diverse mobile kitchens serving everything from organic coffee and fresh juices to barbecued brisket and chicken katsu curry. The pod also boasts substantial vegan and vegetarian options, with a few of the carts, like Native Bowl and Homegrown Smoker, offering a completely meat-free menu; hence, the tofurrito and pulled-pork sandwich stuffers alike amicably share the sizeable covered outdoor dining area between the carts and Prost pub's lively deck.

My top three cart picks are Koi Fusion—hip and happening rolling purveyors of kimchi quesadillas, bulgogi beef sliders, and tacos stuffed with tender shredded grilled short ribs, spicy BBQ pork and sweet soy sauce marinated tofu; Minizo—a mobile ramen and curry shop by the noodle virtuosos behind downtown's popular Shigezo and Division Street's Yataimura Maru; and The Big Egg—their delectable breakfast wrap is your and piglet's just reward for the chilly weekend morning wait.

MUST EATS

Koi's short rib taco and bulgogi beef slider, Minizo's abu ramen and chicken katsu curry, The Big Egg's grilled portobello mushroom and roasted poblano salsa breakfast wrap with ham

SIDE DISH

Prost pub's deck opens onto the heart of Mississippi Marketplace, and you're welcome to come aboard and enjoy your cart meal on the premises, provided you partake of Prost's beverages.

DETAILS

+ Street parking is free and generally easy to find
+ Covered, unheated seating is available

Koi Fusion
SUN, TUE-THU 11am-7pm
FRI-SAT 11am-9pm

HOURS

Minizo
TUE-SUN 11am-3pm

The Big Egg
WED-FRI 8am-1pm
SAT-SUN 9am-1pm

. . . .

4233 N MISSISSIPPI AVENUE
koifusionpdx.com • *facebook.com/pdxminizo*
thebigegg.com

. . . .

$$$$ *Some carts are cash only, ATM on premises*

NATURAL SELECTION

VEGETARIAN/VEGAN *in* CONCORDIA

Considering the relentless consumption I practice on a daily/ hourly basis, I probably wouldn't be alive today to type this with Camembert-covered fingers if I didn't go on a cleanse now and then. You know, a few glasses of green juice/lemon cayenne water in the morning, a big salad for lunch, a colonic and some herbal tea midafternoon, a choucroute garnie for dinner. (Sadly, I never seem to make it more than eight hours when I'm cleansing.)

But in all seriousness, when I'm in the mood to dabble in plant-based dieting without sacrificing presentation, flavor or atmosphere, there's one very obvious foliage-worshipping fine dining destination—this handsome Alberta Street supperhouse, where chef Aaron Woo, inspired by a stint at Napa's revered Ubuntu, crafts gorgeous seasonal tasting menus fit for keeping you on the vegan straight and narrow, a post-cleanse celebration, or just Friday date night with your non-meaty *or* meaty sweetie.

No need to prepare by scanning the menu online and making all tough ordering decisions preemptively so you can relax and enjoy your Sazerac upon arrival, it's really a very simple setup. The $40 prix fixe menu has two columns, A and B, with four dishes in each, all vegetarian, most vegan and gluten-free. Ideally, you get column A, your date gets column B, and you share, but you're free to mix and match or order a la carte at will, so oppositional defiant personality types need not feel constrained by a prix fixe menu authority. Once you've secured your menu of caramelized onion and summer squash soup drizzled with tangerine oil, baby lettuces with figs and sea beans, roasted cauliflower and caponata, and ginger peach cake, it's time to ask yourself that biggest of life questions—to wine pair, or not to wine pair. Yes, you should wine pair. The wine and cocktail list is first-rate, and anyway, everyone knows that a critical part of one's cleanse is at least two glasses of champagne a night.

MUST EATS

The menu changes often, so all you have to do is pick A or B. If necessary, employ eeny, meeny, miny, mo.

SIDE DISH

If you need a venue for your *We Can Stick To A Cleanse For More Than 8 Hours, Dammit!* support group dinner, Natural Selection can be reserved in its entirety, just call to make arrangements, if you aren't already too weak from lack of pork belly sliders, potato chips, and red velvet cake to dial the phone.

DETAILS	HOURS
• Reservations accepted via phone and *opentable.com*	WED-SAT 5:30-10pm
• Street parking is free and generally easy to find	

· ·

3033 NE ALBERTA STREET
503.288.5883 · *naturalselectionpdx.com*

· ·

$$$$ *Credit Cards Accepted*

NED LUDD

NEW AMERICAN *in* KING

Some folks have one tried and true dining love, a restaurant where they take absolutely everyone, from friends and visiting family to colleagues and dates, and this works well for them, except when last Friday's first date runs into them there with this Friday's first date. Other people tailor their eating experiences to their companions' tastes, and I can suggest with utmost confidence that the next time you are supping with a gastronomically-savvy lumberjack, Ned Ludd is your target destination.

Walking in, you're greeted by no fewer than four axes, fitting considering it probably took a lot of chopping to decorate the lovely light-filled dining room, which is a study in the myriad ways one can beautify a space with reclaimed wood. The cornerstone of chef/owner Jason French's concept is the stately wood-fired oven in the center of the open kitchen, and nearly everything on the menu has its moment on the coals—from the pork, beans and chanterelle ragout to the whole roasted trout with charred leeks to perhaps most importantly, the signature inch-thick chocolate chip cookie, which arrives hot from the oven in a salad-plate sized cast iron skillet accompanied by a shot of cold milk. Exempt from the heat are the "Kaltbits," thoughtfully-conceived seasonal vegetable dishes and impeccably-dressed tangles of greens that remind you how perfect a simple salad can be. Wash everything down with a pint of local beer, a glass of E.Z. Orchards cider, a classic cocktail, or maybe just a large tumbler of bourbon, if it was a particularly trying day in the forest. Then climb back on your lumberjack buddy's big blue ox and hit the road.

MUST EATS

Melon and arugula with bacon vinaigrette, pork and bean ragout, Oregon albacore with smoked potato, baked egg in chanterelle cream, giant chocolate chip cookie

SIDE DISH

If your lumberjack has Sundays off, by all means treat them to Ned Ludd's brunch, where you'll sip Krogstad aquavit-laced Ludd's Blood cocktails and feast on stump-sized fresh-baked berry muffins, cornmeal pancakes, and skilletfuls of baked eggs swimming in chanterelle cream. If the weather's agreeable, eat on the roomy picnic-table lined front patio, so you can slip Babe bites of summer vegetable hash.

DETAILS	HOURS
• Reservations accepted via phone and website	WED-SAT 5-10pm
	SUN 5-9pm
• There is a private parking lot, and street parking is free and easy to find	*Brunch*
	SUN 9am-2pm

. . . .

3925 NE MARTIN LUTHER KING BOULEVARD
503.288.6900 • *nedluddpdx.com*

. . . .

**$$$**$ *Credit Cards Accepted*

NOISETTE

FRENCH *in the* ALPHABET DISTRICT

With the exception of the Country Mouse, a little fancy now and then never hurt anybody, so don't let Noisette's promise of being "the fine dining oasis in Portland's sea of casual gastronomy" scare your tattered jeggings off. After all, the gracious hostess greets you in bootcut jeans, cargo-shorts wearing regulars exchange familiar banter with the kitchen crew from their perch at the three-stool bar, and the unlikely location means your patio table comes with an unfettered view of the NW Vaughn Holiday Inn Express. That said, the sommelier wears a well-cut suit, the snow-white tablecloths are starched and pressed, the chandelier and crystal are spit-shined, the champagne has *very* tiny bubbles, and the butter-poached lobster is going to bring tears to your eyes, so by all means, pull your cravat and mother of pearl-handled cane out of mothballs for this meal.

Chef/owner Tony Demes gives you two options, the tasting menu and the chef's tasting menu, and while obviously the menu that starts with the c-word means you're in for a particularly luxe lineup, you'll be more than content with the six-course version, which will save you $35, which you should promptly spend on champagne with very tiny bubbles. Demes' presentation is flawless and color is king—an heirloom tomato soup comes comprised of two contrasting broths, a thin layer of translucent green cucumber geleé supports a dozen miniscule, exactingly-cut squares of root vegetable interspersed with half moons of summer melon while a tidy jumble of Iowa Berkshire prosciutto clings to the side of the bowl, chunks of bright pink, buttery Maine lobster peek from beneath a thatch of yellow and green pole beans, and a thick curl of Spanish octopus sits in a wide smear of charcoal aioli beside rounds of saffron-dyed potato. For dessert, revel in the luxury of a proper chocolate soufflé, served with a small carafe of dark chocolate sauce that's technically for pouring into the soufflé, but, if you've exhausted all your refinement by that point, it goes down just fine as a shot.

MUST EATS

The tasting menu changes often, so you're on your own here.

SIDE DISH

Noisette's wine list is excellent, but if you'd prefer to BYOB, they are happy to open, pour, and even decant your bottle. Corkage fees run from $25 for 750 ml bottles to $200 for 6L Methuselahs. Should you be packing a Balthazar, Nebuchadnezzar, or heaven help us, a Melchizedek, prior approval is required.

DETAILS

- Reservations accepted via phone or *opentable.com*
- Street parking is free and can be difficult to find

HOURS

TUE-SAT 5-10pm

- -

1937 NW 23RD PLACE

503.719.4599 • *noisetterestaurant.com*

- -

$$$$ *Credit Cards Accepted*

NONG'S KHAO MAN GAI

THAI FOOD CART *in* **DOWNTOWN**

The other day, I was half-listening as a friend of mine kept trying to talk to me about how he was a common guy. "Way to embrace mediocrity," I lectured him as I tried to read *Saveur* in peace. He looked at me like I had four ears, which of course, I don't, or I might have been listening to him a little better. "It's hardly mediocre," he said, astonished. "Have you eaten there?" That caught my attention, and henceforth we were able to conduct a more coherent conversation that actually turned out to be about one of downtown Portland's most delicious—and simplest—food carts, Nong's Khao Man Gai.

Standing in front of the neat little red and yellow cart's menu, it won't take you long to make your decision: you can order chicken and rice, or…chicken and rice. But no matter how strongly you feel about choice, you won't feel cheated after you try Nong's one-dish wonder, because she works magic with it—poaching whole free-range chickens with garlic, ginger, salt and sugar until perfectly tender, then adding more ginger, garlic, shallots, and pungent galangal root to the broth and cooking the rice in it.

She slices the chicken up with its fatty skin still on, and serves it on a bed of the seasoned rice, with cucumber slices and cilantro fronds, a side of winter melon soup, and a cup of toffee-colored soybean sauce mixed with, yep, more ginger and garlic, plus a few hot chilies for a little kick. For a scant $7, this all comes wrapped in plain white butcher paper secured with a rubber band. Perfectly simple, yes. But common, it most certainly is not.

MUST EATS
Chicken and rice!

SIDE DISH
Nong is on the move! She opened two more locations at PSU and in Buckman, plans to expand her concept nationally in the next few years, and sells her own line of khao man gai sauce.

DETAILS
- To-go orders can be called in
- Street parking is metered and can be hard to find at the downtown locations; free and generally easy to find at the SE shop

HOURS
SW Alder Location
MON-FRI 10am-4pm
SW College Location
MON-FRI 11am-4pm
SE Location
DAILY 11am-4pm

. . . .

1003 SW ALDER STREET ◆ 971.255.3480
411 SW COLLEGE STREET ◆ 503.432.3286
609 SE ANKENY STREET ◆ 503.740.2907
kmgpdx.com

. . . .

$$$$ *Credit Cards Accepted*

NOSTRANA

ITALIAN *in* BUCKMAN

Nostrana might be one of Portland's prettiest, most popular restaurants, and Cathy Whims might be one of the city's most prolific chefs, and the meticulously assembled Italian-centric wine list might have you pulling out your smart phone and googling a map of Italy and an Italian dictionary, but it's hard to feel intimidated by the impressiveness of it all when you're surrounded by roosters.

There are roosters pecking beneath the big Italian country feast tapestry on the back wall, roosters guarding the hooch at the glossy L-shaped bar, and roosters watching you with sharp little black eyes as you tear into Nostrana's chewy, blistery-crusted signature wood-fired pizzas. The roosters are stuffed of course (nobody wants a bunch of real roosters running around scaring customers and drinking the limoncello), and they add a touch of whimsy to the upscale dining room, reflecting a menu of refined yet rustic Italian cuisine, like the cannellini bean and olive-oil poached albacore salad, grilled pancetta-wrapped Idaho trout, and "straw and hay"—spinach and egg fettuccine with smoked Chinook salmon and golden chanterelles.

For dessert, please don't leave without ordering the melts-on-your-tongue yogurt panna cotta (best in the city, maybe the world) and the heavenly butterscotch budino with salted caramel sauce. Or, order three butterscotch budinos with salted caramel sauce. I think the roosters would approve.

MUST EATS

Insalata Nostrana, capellini with meatballs, rotisserie chicken, margherita pizza, butterscotch budino

SIDE DISH

Both Nostrana and its Pearl District sister pizzeria, Oven & Shaker, have happy hours worth crowing about. At Nostrana's, (nightly, 9pm-close), savor $5 Campari 'n sodas and $6 insalata Nostranas and margheritas. At Oven & Shaker, the early *and* late happy hours offer equally agreeable pizza and cocktail deals.

DETAILS	HOURS
• Reservations accepted via phone or *opentable.com*	*Lunch* MON-FRI . . . 11:30am-2pm
• There is a private parking lot, and street parking is free and easy to find	*Dinner* SUN-THU. . . . . .5-10pm FRI-SAT 5-11pm
	Happy Hour DAILY. 9pm-close

. . . .

1401 SE MORRISON STREET
503.234.2427 • nostrana.com

. . . .

$$$$ *Credit Cards Accepted*

NUESTRA COCINA

MEXICAN *in* HOSFORD-ABERNETHY

Love is great and all, but in my humble opinion, it's Nuestra Cocina's serrano lime drop that makes the world go round. The first sip of this spicy-sweet-tart cocktail, with its sugar-kissed rim and puckery wedge of fresh lime, is colder than a witch's teat and better than a first kiss. Oh yes, it is. And if the serrano lime drop had a soul mate, it would be the kitchen's ceviche of the day—my favorite is the marinated prawns stacked with crispy jicama matchsticks and slices of sweet mango.

The best seat in the house to enjoy this dynamic duo is at the L-shaped mosaic bar overlooking the open kitchen, where you can watch chef/owner Benjamin Gonzalez and crew making crisp black bean and chorizo filled sopes and poblano chiles stuffed with braised squash and Oaxacan cheese. Your meal is preceded by a basket of the same freshly-pressed tortillas used as canvases for the Tacos de Puerco—a steal at $7 for three heaping tacos of tender shredded spiced pork and diced onion. If melted cheese and mushrooms float your love boat, and they really should, ravish the decadent Queso Fundido—a small terracotta cazuela bubbling with baked Spanish cheese and mushrooms in a rich red chili sauce.

Nuestra opens at 5pm and I recommend arriving early—on a good night the wait is 45 minutes, and on a really good night it can be twice that. It must be the serrano lime drops—they're as all-enslaving as true love, but even with the wait, far easier to come by.

MUST EATS

Yucatan lime soup with chicken, pork tacos, tamarind-marinated prawns, BBQ lamb shoulder, crepes with cinnamon cream

SIDE DISH

If you've ever wished you could cook like the dynamos behind the stoves at Nuestra, you can at least try—once a month, a member of the kitchen staff teaches an evening cooking class. Or, book a private class for you and 11 of your closest friends.

DETAILS	HOURS
• No reservations	TUE-SAT 5-10pm
• Street parking is free and generally easy to find	

. . . .

2135 SE DIVISION STREET

503.232.2135 ◆ *nuestra-cocina.com*

. . . .

**$$**$$ *Credit Cards Accepted*

NUVREI

BAKERY *in the* PEARL DISTRICT

"Happiness is a ham and cheese croissant," promised the sandwich board sitting on the sidewalk outside Nuvrei. I happen to think happiness is a chilled bottle of bubbly, a cheese and chouquette-filled picnic basket, and a lazy spring afternoon in the Versailles gardens, but I gamely followed the smell of sugar, spice and everything nice into master baker Marius Pop's beautiful light-filled lair in the heart of Portland's posh Pearl District.

If it's breakfast, or even if it isn't, indulge in a feathery cinnamon danish kissed with rum and orange oil, flaky cherry walnut or chocolate orange scone, plum brioche, and flourless chewy chocolate cookie—the inky lovechild of an elemental threesome: egg whites, confectioners' sugar, and cocoa powder. Then there are the croissants—stuffed with almond paste, dripping with dark chocolate, or harboring fat slices of Black Forest ham and creamy béchamel sauce and topped with a crunchy golden dusting of toasted Emmentaler cheese, they can easily transform a lackluster morning into something out of a Parisian dream.

If you don't feel like leaving, even after your second croissant and cappuccino, you shouldn't, after all, Nuvrei's lunch offerings could easily sustain you all afternoon. Settle in with the rich croque-madame or monsieur, a salmon and cucumber layered house bagel, or an Oregon bay shrimp, avocado and apricot crème fraîche croissant sandwich. For dessert, well, by now you've probably been eyeing the radiant rows of macarons long enough to select an ideal mix. Nibbling the pistachio, one can't help but think…who says you can't buy happiness?!

MUST EATS

Almond croissant, plum brioche, chewy chocolate walnut cookie, smoked cheddar and wild salmon pretzel, shrimp avocado sandwich

SIDE DISH

Morning work meetings are terribly dull things, unless of course you're the shining star who brings a platter of Nuvrei's petite pastries—perfect miniature reproductions of their best baked delicacies. Order platters by calling 503.546.3032 or emailing *order@nuvrei.com*, and don't blame me if you get a raise.

DETAILS	HOURS
• No reservations	MON-SAT....... 7am-5pm
• Street parking is free and generally easy to find	SUN 8am-5pm

. . . .

404 NW 10TH AVENUE

503.972.1700 • *nuvrei.com*

. . . .

$$$$ *Credit Cards Accepted*

THE OCEAN

MICRORESTAURANT COLLECTIVE *in* KERNS

There was no picky eating in the Stevenson household, because picky eaters got two choices for dinner—eat what was on the table, or go muck out the chicken coop. Option A, while not always the popular candidate, enjoyed 100% of the vote. Of course, not everyone has a chicken coop with which to combat picky eating, but from what I can tell, many Portland parents have come up with a far more civilized solution: they simply haul the whole gang down to The Ocean—NE Glisan's novel collective of four microrestaurants, a pie shop, and a deli/butcher shop—stick their family flag into a picnic table on the communal patio, and let everyone and their meal money loose.

Some will head for the agua fresca and salsa drenched shores of azure-walled Uno Más taqueria, to indulge in platefuls of fresh tacos heaped with everything from carnitas to tender sautéed cactus, or pool their resources for the Taquiza Surtida—a dozen chef's choice tacos for a flat $20. Others, probably the teenagers, will go next door to cheerful 24th & Meatballs, whether for the saucy meatball heroes and hot waffle balls with dulce de leche dipping sauce, or to giggle over the saucy mottos ("Portland's tastiest balls," "Put our balls in your mouth," etc), it's hard to say. And others will scatter to the west end of the complex—returning with trays weighted down with Slowburger's smoked bacon, tomato relish and sweet and sour iceberg slaw-topped sliders and sea salt French fries (stinky cheese optional). In the meantime, Dad's down at Tails & Trotters deli procuring a porkstrami sandwich while Mom's indulging in a marionberry piehole at Pie Spot, or sometimes, they're both just sitting at the table in a tired daze, hungrily eyeing the wine bar across the street. After the ensuing upscale food court feeding frenzy has subsided, everyone tosses their dishes in the respective bus tubs and heads home, neatly sidestepping any potential dish duty arguments. Which in the Stevenson household, were met with two choices—do the dishes, or....well, you know.

MUST EATS

Slowburger's pancetta, blue cheese and tomato relish burger, Uno Más' pastor and moronga tacos, 24th & Meatball's Italian balls with hazelnut arugula pesto, Pie Spot's chocolate peanut butter piehole, Tails & Trotters' porkstrami on rye

SIDE DISH

All six Ocean eateries have indoor seating, four have alcoholic beverages, and one has hot waffle balls.

DETAILS	HOURS
• No reservations	DAILY........11am-11pm
• Street parking is free and generally easy to find	*Hours vary by establishment, check their websites for detailed info*

. . . .

NE 24TH AVENUE & NE GLISAN STREET

unomastaquiza.com • *24thandmeatballs.com*

slowburger.net • *pie-spot.com* • *tailsandtrotters.com*

. . . .

$$$$ *Credit Cards Accepted*

OLD SALT MARKETPLACE

NEW AMERICAN *in* **CONCORDIA**

We all have one of those days where we feel like there isn't enough variety in our lives. We've been at the same fortune cookie-writing job for a year, with the same spouse for six long months, drinking the same keg of beer for a week, listening to the same Lonely Island song on repeat for four hours. We need some kind of interesting, mind-expanding adventure, via legal channels, and obviously, involving a lot of good food.

Old Salt Marketplace to the rescue! The Grain & Gristle trio's second project, this stylishly aw-shucks collaborative unites a supperhouse, bar, deli, butcher shop, bakery, cooking school, farmers' market, commissary kitchen and vermouth distillery under one wide roof. Is that enough variety for you? Okay, good, here we go. Take Thursday afternoon off, and at 1pm, walk through the deli door, order a Reuben on rye, a cup of Chuckwagon chili, and a half pound of kale lentil salad (for your health). At 2pm, proceed to adjoining Miss Zumstein bakery for one of brilliant bakeress Anja Spence's pastries, perhaps a lemon cream tartlet or cappuccino brownie and a cup of Extracto coffee. Rest, and repeat. At 4pm, pop outside and have a stroll around the weekly farmers' market in the parking lot. Eat a Fressen pretzel, do some brazen people-watching, pet a small wiry terrier of questionable friendliness, feel the blood pumping in your veins! At 5pm, the clock hits Cocktail Hour, so head inside for an Old Salt Old Fashioned and the house pork rinds. At 6pm, your lamb butchery class with chef Ben

Meyer starts at chef Blake Van Roekel's Good Keuken cooking school, and when you emerge at 9pm, bloodied and triumphant, with a pound of lamb ribs in your handbag, it's dinnertime. You start with a pint of Upright Seven and salt cod fritters, move on to the roasted half chicken with fried green tomato panzanella salad, and end with peach upside down cake and a Manhattan crafted with house-bottled vermouth. Staggering to your cab at midnight, you reflect on the day—horizons-busting, buzz-inducing, totally legal. *And* you've got lamb ribs for a 2am snack!

MUST EATS

Cherry tomato and tuna salad, pole beans with soft egg, meat pie, roasted half chicken, peach upside down cake

SIDE DISH

For a slightly less involved culinary adventure, try Old Salt's Let Us Cook For You menu. Name your price ($25+), and the kitchen sends out a mystery menu, omakase-style.

DETAILS	HOURS
• Reservations accepted for parties of eight or more	*Supperhouse & Bar* DAILY 5pm-12am
• Street parking is free and easy to find	*Meat Shop & Deli* DAILY 11am-7pm

. . . .

5027 NE 42ND AVENUE

971.255.0167 • oldsaltpdx.com

. . . .

**$$**$$ *Credit Cards Accepted*

OLYMPIC PROVISIONS

NEW AMERICAN *in the* ALPHABET DISTRICT/BUCKMAN

Portland is full of interesting secrets—secret catacombs, secret kebabs, secret gardens, and Secret Society, to name a few. Then there are Olympic Provisions' restaurants, which aren't technically secrets, but unless you're a particularly thorough wanderer, prone to getting lost, or have business in the industrial wilds of Southeast and Northwest Portland, you'd be hard-pressed to stumble upon either one. So, switch on your pâté-dar and follow the scent of smoked Sweetheart hams to these hip, handsome meat meccas, where you'll find two distinct culinary identities, faultless wine lists, and *plenty* of animal protein.

Immediately upon entering the Northwest restaurant, you'll encounter one of the city's finest meat counters—brimming with sausages, frankfurters, pâtés, rillettes, bacon, and OP's acclaimed salami, produced in-house by salumist Eli Cairo and his hard-working team. Take a seat at the marble bar overlooking chef Colin Stafford's compact, briskly-efficient kitchen, and pair a dozen oysters with sparkling Vouvray, or take over a boisterous communal table and share one of the incomparable rotisserie chickens and a heap of Schmaltz potatoes with friends.

Or, for a sexy candlelit supper with someone you like to share your meat with, hone in on the Southeast location, marked with OP's trademark blinking MEAT sign, and home to chef Alex Yoder's exceptional menu of Mediterranean-influenced small plates. Although the menu certainly toes the company's "Meat

Here" line, punctuated by hearty pork rillette hand pies, braised short ribs, and beef carpaccio, I've never plunged my fork into a vegetable dish I didn't love. Add in the infallible wall of wine and swoony desserts, and it's just the spot to seal the deal, especially if you reserve the "Nook," a dark, romantic, secluded booth tucked beneath the stairs, that's just perfect for secret canoodling.

MUST EATS

Spanish charcuterie board, braised octopus salad, roast chicken, rotisserie prime rib, chocolate salami

SIDE DISH

Besides being refreshingly line-free in a town that prides itself on weekend morning waits, OP's brunches offer an incomparable Sweetheart ham Benedict and kielbasa hash, and don't even get me started on the chocolate chip pancakes with orange butter.

DETAILS	HOURS
• Reservations accepted via phone or *opentable.com*	*NW Location* DAILY . . . . Hours vary
• Street parking is free and generally easy to find	*SE Location* DAILY . . . . Hours vary

· ·

1632 NW THURMAN STREET · 503.894.8136
107 SE WASHINGTON STREET · 503.954.3663
olympicprovisions.com

· ·

**$$$**$ *Credit Cards Accepted*

OX

I have a friend who inputs everything she eats into a calorie tracking tool, which she is required to show to her gym's boot camp instructor, a stern, disciplined sort of guy who thinks lemon-infused water is a food group and ordering one of each dessert is a *bad* thing. But because, like me, she suffers a total lack of self control when confronted by a bewitching menu's siren call, and neither of us has the good sense to lash ourselves to the grocery store produce case or refrigerator crisper drawer, like Odysseus, after our last meal at Ox, she had to go into hiding.

Because strangely enough, when we typed in "sunchoke and Oregon black truffle empanada, Dungeness crab bruschetta, clam chowder with marrow bone, smoked beef tongue with sweetbread croutons, 8 oz. skirt steak, lamb T-bone, coals-roasted artichoke with Espelette mayo, lobster mushroom risotto, heirloom hominy with braised pork belly and fried duck egg, and grilled escarole gratin with bagna cauda cream," followed by a cheese board and five desserts (one of each, obviously), the calorie tracker gave a deep sigh, high-fived us, and shut down forever. But really, exile is a small price to pay for a magnificent meal at chefs Greg Denton and Gabrielle Quiñónez Denton's marvelous, much-loved Argentine-inspired stronghold of beef and bones. You won't find a warmer, more convivial table in town, be you at the counter facing the massive, fragrant, wood-fired grill that is the heart and soul of the restaurant, or on a comfy banquette bench across from the busy bar, and the welcoming spirit applies to eaters of all persuasions—despite the restaurant's meaty rep, it's quite sensitive to herbivores and much of the menu is gluten-free, including one of the best desserts, a hazelnut brown butter torte with honey chamomile ice cream. And so, a few hours, a few cocktails, and a few billion calories later, head home smelling of wood smoke, pack a valise, and hop a plane to Buenos Aires—my friend will be happy to show you around her new city.

MUST EATS

Smoked beef tongue with sweetbread croutons, clam chowder, five seafood preparations, lamb T-bone, hazelnut brown butter torte

SIDE DISH

During peak times, Ox waits can be as formidable as the 36 oz. ribeye—so take a seat in their charming neighboring Whey Bar and brave one of the infamous Dirty Grandma Agnes cocktails, which also comes in a 4-serving Mason jar if it's that kinda night.

DETAILS

- Reservations accepted for parties of six or more
- There is a private parking lot, and street parking is free and easy to find

HOURS

SUN, TUE-THU . . 5-10pm
FRI-SAT 5-11pm

. . . .

2225 NE MARTIN LUTHER KING JR BLVD
503.284.3366 • *oxpdx.com*

. . . .

$$$$ *Credit Cards Accepted*

PAADEE

THAI *in* KERNS

We can all learn a lesson from the classic movie *The Birdcage*, courtesy of the loveably inept Agador Spartacus, a man who, if you think about it, could have averted a considerable amount of stress if he'd just ordered Thai food instead of making Guatemalan Peasant Soup.

I think that deep thought sometimes (Jack Handey has nothing on me) as I'm sitting in equally loveable restaurateur Earl Ninsom's beautiful Thai restaurant, watching the decorative birdcages overhead swing slightly in the breeze drifting through the wide windows facing Portland's bustling and aptly-named Restaurant Row. Ninsom imported them from his native Thailand, along with all the furniture, dishware, and many of the recipes that punctuate his sophisticated menu of snacks, noodles, soups, salads and plates, which are joined by a half dozen signature craft cocktails, whose easy drinkability coupled with the long communal tables in the center of the dining room make for interesting random interactions over chive cakes, Sriracha and fish sauce-glazed fried chicken wings, grilled hanger steak with spicy tamarind dip, and bowls of hot noodles. Early eaters and budgeteers, PaaDee's well-rounded happy hour is one of the city's best—choose from a handful of $6 cocktails, then make a substantial meal out of the deeply discounted appetizers and $5 noodle dishes.

MUST EATS

Fried Sriracha and fish sauce wings, Chinese chive cakes, ba mee "Pitsanulok," khao soi, hanger steak with sticky rice

SIDE DISH

Less than two miles away, sharing a food-blessed Buckman block with Trifecta, Bunk, and Robo Taco, is Earl's third venture, Tarad, a charming, casual noodle joint with embedded miniature Asian market. Have a plate of guay tiew kua gai, buy all the exoticisms needed to craft a homemade Thai feast, then, six hours and six Singhas later, if it didn't quite work out, concede defeat, wash the fish sauce out of your bangs, and return for takeout, just like Agador Spartacus should have done.

DETAILS	HOURS
• Reservations accepted via phone	DAILY 11:30am-3pm
	. . . . 5-10pm
• Street parking is free and generally easy to find	*Happy Hour*
	DAILY 5-6:30pm

6 SE 28TH AVENUE

503.360.1453 • *paadeepdx.com*

**$$**$$ *Credit Cards Accepted*

PACIFIC PIE COMPANY

PIE in HOSFORD-ABERNETHY/NORTHWEST

I'm a bit embarrassed to admit that before Pacific Pie Company came to town, my knowledge of savory pies was largely confined to the supermarket frozen food section. But savory pies are huge in Australia—land of Vegemite, Tim Tams, Lamingtons, Shrimp on the Barbie, and perhaps tastiest of the lot, Hugh Jackman—and thankfully, Pacific Pie Company bakers/owners Sarah Curtis-Fawley and Chris Powell (an honest-to-goodness Australian native with the irresistible accent to match) have given me and the rest of Portland a thorough education in the nuances of Down Under-style pie.

Sarah and Chris, who learned to make savory pies from the most famous pie purveyor in Australia, Old Stone Hut Bakery, run bustling restaurants in Northwest and Southeast Portland, where they sell both freshly-baked and frozen pies for eat-in or eat-later—beef and stout pie, roast lamb pie, curried lentil pie, creamy chicken pie, black bean and Jack pie...all enrobed in Sarah's tender, flaky butter crust and topped with a little pastry cutout identifying the goodness within (the chicken pie has a tiny pastry chicken on top, the lamb pie has a tiny pastry lamb on top, the beef and mushroom pie has...well, you get it).

They also bake deliciously authentic pulled pork and spinach feta pasties, plump sausage rolls, Lamingtons, and a dessert that's immediately recognizeable no matter which side of the equator you're on—*sweet* pies, like carmelized pear and hazelnut, apple sour cream streusel, and chocolate peanut butter. Sorry Hugh Jackman, you're perfectly lovely and everything, but I've decided that *pie* is Australia's tastiest import.

MUST EATS

Beef and stout pie, Sunday roast lamb pie, Moroccan chickpea pasty, sausage roll, peanut butter chocolate pie

SIDE DISH

Twice a month, Sarah and PPC Pastry Chef Kate Withiam teach Pie 101, an intimate hands-on class that schools you in the art of piemaking, then sends you home with a fresh-baked pie.

DETAILS

+ No reservations
+ Street parking is free and generally easy to find

HOURS

SE Location
DAILY.......... 11am-9pm
NW Location
DAILY......... 11am-11pm
Happy Hour
MON-FRI 3-6pm

. . . .

1520 SE 7TH AVENUE + 503.381.6157
1668 NW 23RD AVENUE + 503.894.9482
pacificpieco.com

. . . .

$$$$ *Credit Cards Accepted*

PALEY'S PLACE

FRENCH *in the* **ALPHABET DISTRICT**

I'll admit it—when my parents come to town, I still get excited when they offer to take me anywhere I want for dinner, on their dime. How do you ever outgrow the allure of an extravagantly indulgent no-budgetary-strings-attached supper, the kind where you overorder with wild abandon and don't feel one morsel of guilt for the two pre-dinner cocktails and three desserts? I don't think you do. So when my parents arrive and the offer is made, I make a beeline for Paley's Place, one of Portland's most esteemed fine-dining establishments, housed in a plush, elegantly-restored Victorian in Northwest Portland. Owner Kimberly Paley graciously seats us among the lovey-dovey couples celebrating landmark life events and the oenophiles exercising their expense accounts, and I immediately order an Apple Brandy Smash—a concoction of Applejack brandy, Lillet Rose and muddled mint, and begin to plot the perfect meal.

It might start with a half dozen Kumamoto oysters, chef/owner Vitaly Paley's classic steak tartare and the crispy sweetbreads with orange-glazed fennel, followed by grilled pork loin and tomato and white bean stew, or cedar-plank Columbia River salmon. Or, if I'm feeling particularly ravenous and posh—the epic dry-aged grass-fed Wilson Ranch ribeye with foie gras hollandaise. I'll end the evening with a wedge of one of my favorite Oregon cheeses—Ancient Heritage Dairy's soft-ripened Adelle, and one of pastry chef Michelle Vernier's divine desserts—like the classic crème brûlée, warm chocolate soufflé cake with honey vanilla ice cream, or apple dumpling with caramel corn (or, since my mother shares my inability to make tough dessert decisions—all three). The fat lady (me, by this point) of Epicurean Extravagance sings over a digestif of Clear Creek Pear Brandy, and then it's back out into the cold, cruel, real world of tartare-less, one-dessert dining.

MUST EATS

Steak tartare, sweetbreads, Maine diver scallops, Paley's burger, chocolate soufflé cake

SIDE DISH

Chef Paley also opened two downtown restaurants with former Beaker & Flask Chef Ben Bettinger—swanky Imperial, with exceptional service and a superb cocktail and wine list, and the casual Portland Penny Diner, a neighboring corner cafe specializing in elevated comfort food like duck bologna breakfast sandwiches and Reuben croissants.

DETAILS	HOURS	
• Reservations accepted	MON-THU	5:30-10pm
• Street parking is free and generally easy to find	FRI-SAT	5-11pm
	SUN	5-10pm
	Happy Hour	
	DAILY	Opening-6:30pm

....

1204 NW 21ST AVENUE

503.243.2403 • *paleysplace.net*

....

$$$$ *Credit Cards Accepted*

PARK KITCHEN

NEW AMERICAN *in the* **PEARL DISTRICT**

When stuck in a seemingly endless food festival line, I alleviate the tedium by silently playing the "If You Could Only Eat One Thing Until The End of Time, What Would It Be?" game. Coming in a close second to "spoonfuls of melted chocolate" is the Park Kitchen flank steak salad. A permanent fixture on the menu, probably because there would be a patron revolt, complete with a few bocce balls from the adjacent court being sent through the front window if they ever took it off, it is the perfect meal—tender strips of flank steak gently tossed with creamy blue cheese, crisp Italian parsley, and sherried onions. It's exactly the sort of dish chef/owner Scott Dolich and his team excel at: simple, true to the ingredients, and relentlessly flavorful.

A perennial Portland favorite, Park Kitchen lies in a remodeled historic building across from the north end of the tree-lined, bocce-endowed North Park Blocks, and when the weather is cordial, its handful of umbrella-shaded sidewalk tables are prime dining real estate. The four-table front room cuddles up against a roll-up garage door overlooking the park, separated from the intimate yet convivial back dining room and open kitchen by a sleek copper bar—an excellent spot to sip skillfully-mixed cocktails while you wait for a table or decompress after a long day at the office. The devotedly seasonal menu entices with inventive dishes like chilled corn soup with clams, pole beans and roasted plums, and Oregon albacore with tomatillos. Or, if your entire table is agreeable, spring for one of the chef's tasting menus—the kitchen will send out a diverse spread of family-style dishes. Dessert's more fun (and a lot better smelling) than a gaggle of old Italian men playing bocce, so don't pass up the summer berry trifle or double chocolate tart with salted caramel and Oregon hazelnut ice cream.

MUST EATS

Flank steak salad, sherry-cured anchovies, warm chanterelle custard, roasted pork with red-eye gravy, double chocolate tart

SIDE DISH

Scott Dolich's second project, a Northwest Portland gastropub called The Bent Brick, occupies the ivy-covered brick building at the corner of NW 17th and Marshall, and serves a duck fat jojo-endowed happy hour Tuesday through Sunday.

DETAILS	HOURS
• Reservations accepted via phone or *opentable.com*	DAILY.............5-9pm
	Happy Hour
• Street parking is metered and generally easy to find	DAILY.............5-6pm

. . . .

422 NW 8TH AVENUE

503.223.7275 • *parkkitchen.com*

. . . .

**$$$**$ *Credit Cards Accepted*

PDX671

GUAMANIAN FOOD CART *in* ROSE CITY PARK

Thanks to my mother's devout health food leanings, we kids thought there were only three food groups—carrot raisin salad, pinto beans, and sprouted things. A young gourmand, I was not. So if you'd arrived via tesseract and told my 12-year-old sprouted-toast wielding self that someday I'd write books extolling the virtues of a giant silver Guamanian food truck's chicken thighs, I'd have squinted at you through my thick glasses, asked if you had any contraband Starburst, and gone back to reading *A Wrinkle In Time*.

But life is funny, so here I am, penning a love letter about chicken thighs, specifically, the celestial marinated and grilled Chamorro chicken thighs that are the cornerstone of PDX671 chef/owner Edward Calvo Sablan's menu. If you order the Fiesta Plate, which comes with a chicken thigh, light and airy corn-specked Oregon shrimp fritter, and annatto-seed tinted "red rice" plus the spicy-salty-sour-sweet house finadene sauce, you'll be able to sample half the cart's short and sweet menu in one go. But don't stop there, for my heart belongs to the Kelaguen Mannok—neatly-chopped grilled chicken thigh tossed with diced celery, onion, coconut, lemon and small, hot chilis, and served with wedges of titiyas, a warm, soft, ultra-satisfying handmade coconut milk flatbread. It is one of the simplest, but most enchanting dishes you'll ever eat, whether you were raised as a culinary savant or shared my sprouted fate.

MUST EATS

Shrimp fritters, lumpia, kelaguen mannok, titiyas, cucumber salad

SIDE DISH

PDX671 is part of the Rose City Food Park cart pod, a community of 13 lucky carts and a Kruger's farm stand located in a brightly bemuraled lot on NE Sandy Boulevard. If you have time/room, visit the Moberi cart, which sells fresh juice blends with names like Trampled By Turtles and Affordable Healthcare, protein drinks, and smoothies made via a bicycle blender that you have the option of pedaling yourself. Or, if you're craving something baked, not blended, slip up the street to lovely baker/author Kim Boyce's marvelous Bakeshop bakery.

DETAILS

+ Street parking is free and relatively easy to find

HOURS

TUE-SAT . . . . Hours vary

. . . .

5221 NE SANDY BOULEVARD

971.570.0945 · *pdx671.com*

. . . .

$$$$ *Credit Cards Accepted*

PEARL BAKERY

BAKERY *in the* PEARL DISTRICT

There must be 50 ways to leave your lover, but there are at least 50,000 ways to eat a Pearl Bakery chocolate panini, my favorite being to stand at the long, narrow Parisian-style wood-slab counter and slather this moist little puck of just-baked chocolate bread with raspberry jam, paying no mind to the melty bits of chocolate getting all over my hands, face and dress. Chocolate on my snout is nothing new.

A beautiful bastion of all things mixed, fermented, kneaded and baked, Eric and Mary Lester's Pearl District bakery has high ceilings, old-fashioned tiled floors, a sprinkling of bistro tables, and a large glowing doorway that affords a glimpse of the huge commercial ovens and mountains of flour sacks in their production space, which gives new meaning to the phrase "see the light." It also has a pastry selection that may cause you to start your day with an unsightly drool patch on your crisp white work shirt, thanks to the piles and platters of cinnamon crowns, espresso walnut brownies, pistachio apricot macarons, lemon crème fraiche cakes, and huckleberry fromage blanc tarts.

On a fair summer morning, take an hour before work and order a cup of Batdorf & Bronson coffee and an almond croissant or candied orange peel studded gibassier, claim a sidewalk table, and read or watch passerby—it's one of the Portland life's greatest little joys. In winter, substitute the sidewalk setting for an indoor bistro table and carry on as before.

Should you need a sandwich fix come noon, Pearl Bakery serves homemade sandwiches on the freshest of bread, and if the winter sleet has frozen your nose hairs solid, you might want a cup of tomato basil soup as well, for thawing and warming purposes, and to dip your chocolate panini in.

MUST EATS

All of the croissants, cinnamon crown, gibassier, chocolate panini, smoked turkey sandwich with cream cheese and avocado

SIDE DISH

Like it wasn't enough that they'd hooked you on their chocolate panini, Pearl Bakery went and started their own line of Pearl Chocolates. Handcrafted by chocolatier Teresa Ulrich, the gorgeous collection of small-batch truffles, bonbons and bars can be found at the bakery, Cacao, and both Pastaworks markets.

DETAILS	HOURS
• No reservations	MON-FRI... 6:30am-5:30pm
• Street parking is metered	SAT 7am-5pm
and generally easy to find	SUN 8am-3pm

. . . .

102 NW 9TH AVENUE

503.827.0910 • *pearlbakery.com*

. . . .

$$$$ *Credit Cards Accepted*

PIAZZA ITALIA

ITALIAN *in the* PEARL DISTRICT

"He looked just like an angel," my mom said dreamily, staring off into the distance. "Who? Dad?" I asked skeptically, looking at my dad, who was peering over his spectacles at his E-trade account, grimacing at the laptop and not looking much like an angel at all. "The boy who brought my pasta at that little Italian restaurant you sent us to," she gushed. "He had these golden curls that framed his face, and they glowed when the sunlight hit them, like a halo, and he looked just like an angel." She sighed rapturously. "And the spaghetti mare, it was delicious... the sauce was so fragrant, the pasta was so fresh...it was just like in Orvieto, remember, at that little trattoria?"

Suddenly, I understood—my mom had been bitten by the Piazza Italia bug and was certifiably smitten, which I've noticed, is nothing new. When my favorite Brits, Matt and Sian, lived here, they were simply mad about Piazza Italia. It reminded them of their weekend jaunts to Italy—the pasta, the wine, the accents, the bickering, the World Cup games on the television.

It's hard not to be taken with this festive family-owned Italian joint, with its inimitable atmosphere, well-stocked wine wall, and satisfying homemade pastas like the creamy proscuitto and black pepper laced linguine squarchiarella and hearty lasagna with bechamel. Start your meal with the antipasto Italiano plate—grilled vegetables, beans, and smoked salmon, or the bruschetta Monferrin, piled high with sauteed mushrooms tossed with pancetta and garlic. Order a bottle of Barolo off the 100% Italian-wine list, and linger over tiramisu so you can soak up this engaging slice of Italian life just a little bit longer.

MUST EATS

Minestrone soup, antipasto Italiano, pappardelle with wild boar ragu, bucatini with pancetta, linguine with egg and prosciutto

SIDE DISH

Soccer fans, this is your mecca. Your passion for field footsie is shared by the staff, who always seem to have a match playing on the television. And when the World Cup rolls around, the ardent uprising of emotion exuded by the faithful crowd of regulars can nearly topple your table.

DETAILS

- Reservations accepted
- Street parking is metered and can be difficult to find

HOURS

DAILY	11:30am-3pm
MON-THU	5-10pm
FRI-SAT	5-11pm
SUN	5-9pm

. . . .

1129 NW JOHNSON STREET
503.478.0619 • piazzaportland.com

. . . .

**$$$**$ *Credit Cards Accepted*

PINE STATE BISCUITS

BISCUITS *in* CONCORDIA/HOSFORD-ABERNETHY

There are few things as painful as waiting in line at the Pine State Biscuits booth at Portland Farmers' Market for 37 minutes and then, just as you eagerly step up to the front of the line, being told that the person before you got the very last biscuit. Once upon a time, there was no recourse for this situation other than stalking that person and their biscuit, bopping them over the head with a butternut squash, and taking what was unrightfully yours, but that was messy, immoral, and illegal.

Nowadays, Pine State Biscuits owners Walt Alexander, Kevin Atchley and Brian Snyder—all North Carolina natives who started this venture from a shared love and longing for real Southern-style buttermilk biscuits—have two charming biscuit cafés, so you can circumvent the farmers' market biscuit roulette and second-degree assault and biscuit theft charges by visiting either of their locations, diplomatically located in both Southeast and Northeast Portland.

The succinct menu is chock-full of biscuit sandwiches made with fresh, local ingredients, from The Moneyball—a basic structure of egg and gravy, to the famous Reggie Deluxe—a giant piece of crispy fried chicken dogpiled by a fried egg, bacon and cheese, in a pool of gravy, a creation so decadent, it was featured on Oprah's "Sandwich Showdown." Once you've gone that far calorically, might as well make it a home run of gluttony, so go ahead and order the hash ups—crisp golden hash browns with country ham, grilled onions, mushrooms and cheese, plus a pecan Pie Spot pie hole and a tall glass of

Xocolatl de David's Champ's Chocolate Milk. Sure, you'll be in a food coma for hours afterwards, but at least you and your butternut squash accomplice will have clean consciences.

MUST EATS

Reggie Deluxe, Pine State Fried Club, The Moneyball, hash ups, fried green tomatoes

SIDE DISH

Just because you don't have to wait in line for a Pine State Biscuits sandwich at the Portland Farmers' Market anymore doesn't mean you can't—their booth serves up freshly-made biscuit sandwiches rain or shine, all season long.

DETAILS

+ No reservations
+ Street parking is free and generally easy to find

HOURS

DAILY......... Hours vary

· ·

2204 NE ALBERTA STREET ✦ 503.477.6605
1100 SE DIVISION STREET *(Opening winter 2013)*
pinestatebiscuits.com

· ·

$$$$ *Credit Cards Accepted*

PIP'S ORIGINAL

DOUGHNUTS *in* **CULLY**

Sadly, I wasn't born with the gene that makes one relish strenuous exercise, but I *was* born with whatever gene makes you want to eat doughnuts and kielbasa 12 times a day (sometimes, but not always, together). So, in an attempt to counterbalance this genetic feud, I've developed Destination Exertion strategies, the best of which is the Doughnut Dash. The premise is simple, decide how long or far you'd like to walk/run/bike/lunge/rollerblade/hop-on-one-foot, then carefully map out a route that bypasses as many doughnut shops as possible. It's far more entertaining than a doughnut-less gym, and best of all, it gives you a reason to hop on one foot to Pip's Original every morning.

Owners Nate and Jamie Snell have kept things elementary, my dear Destination Exerter, by doing one thing and doing it more than well—miniature, made-to-order doughnuts. Roughly the circumference and thickness of an activity tracking wristband, these soft, spice-flecked confections fry to golden sublimity right in front of your eyes, before being drizzled with Nutella, rolled in cinnamon sugar, or, in their most superlative incarnation, given a raw honey bath and dusted with pink Himalayan sea salt. While it's true that you can't really improve on perfection, you *can* put ice cream on it, so Pip's does just that, resulting in the Alameda, a scoop of local Cloud City caramelized banana ice cream set atop a warm cinnamon sugar doughnut, then carefully capped with a spiral of Nutella. Coupled with one of Pip's signature housemade chai tea lattes (which can be dirtied up with a shot of Extracto espresso, for extra oomph), it's enough to stop even the most determined marathoner in their tracks. Which prompts this parting advice—if you plan on your Doughnut Dash having more than one stop, hit Pip's last.

MUST EATS

There are only five or so doughnut-related menu items, so just order a dozen of each

SIDE DISH

Every now and then, Pip's announces a "Flash Free Special" on their Facebook page, which involves you spending five dollars or so within a prescribed window of time, and getting a dozen free hot fresh miniature doughnuts in return. It is easily the best reason to check your Facebook feed every 10 minutes.

DETAILS	HOURS
• No reservations	TUE-SUN 8am-4pm
• Street parking is free and easy to find	

. . . .

4759 NE FREMONT STREET
503.206.8692 • *pipsoriginal.com*

. . . .

$$$$ *Credit Cards Accepted*

PIX/BAR VIVANT

DESSERT/TAPAS BAR *in* KERNS

Historically, split personalities have gotten a bad rap, no thanks to Dr. Jekyll and Mr. Hyde, The Incredible Hulk, Mister Negative, and of course, treacherous little Gollum. But split personalities *completely* redeem themselves at Cheryl Wakerhauser's beautiful Burnside establishment—part French café like the kind where impeccably-dressed Parisians sip fine champagne and nibble luxurious desserts and chocolates (aka Pix Patisserie), part San Sebastian-style tapas bar like the kind where porrons flow freely all night long and rowdy Spaniards throw their napkins on the floor when they've finished their pintxos (aka Bar Vivant).

Separated by a curved bar dubbed the "Pyrenees," Pix and Bar Vivant work quite well together despite their differences— order an array of tiny tapas at the bar, then either eat them authentically (standing up, followed by the aforementioned napkin-tossing), or ask the staff to ferry them to a café table so you can dine beneath the epic wall of empty bubbly bottles. If you opt to go directly to the Pix side of things, soak in the eclectic oh-lá-lá decor—think crimson damask wallpaper, flickering votives, a case of desserts and confections so pretty it's almost criminal to eat them, and a merrily decadent spirit— there isn't a better place to find your joie de vivre *and* a serious sugar high. Possibilities are endless—convene with girlfriends to swap tales of sultry European summer flings over Calvados and pear tartlets blanketed in milk chocolate rosemary ganache, play pétanque and drink cider on the patio, book an elegant Sunday afternoon tea, or just cozy up with your sweetheart, a Queen of Sheba truffle cake, two spoons, a bottle of very good champagne, and an arsenal of sweet nothings to whisper intermittently. Split personalities have never been quite so versatile, or so delicious.

MUST EATS

Amelie, Shazam, drunken cherries, one of each macaron, nougat

SIDE DISH

Few places throw a party like Pix, so don't miss their annual Fête du Macaron, dessert Dim Sum Yum Yum, Bubbly Spectacular, and raucous New Year's Eve and Bastille Day Block parties. Check the website or Facebook to get the good times updates.

DETAILS

- Reservations accepted for parties of six or more
- Street parking is free and relatively easy to find

HOURS

SUN-THU...... 2pm-12am
FRI-SAT 2pm-2am
Happy Hour
DAILY.............. 2-4pm

· ·

2225 E BURNSIDE STREET
971.271.7166 · *pixpatisserie.com*

· ·

$$$$ *Credit Cards Accepted*

POD 28

FOOD CART POD *in* BUCKMAN

Just like children, old cars, and capuchin monkeys, each Portland cart pod has a distinct personality, and I think of Pod 28 as the Sunday Afternoon Pod, mostly because all of the carts are open on Sunday afternoon, and really, what better use of your day off than sitting on your tuffet within a hop's throw of the Captured By Porches beer bus, eating your tortas and pappardelle?

Congregating on the lick of Buckman asphalt between Vino wine shop and Crema coffeehouse, these food cart kids on the Restaurant Row block casually circle a jumble of tables and a crooked row of old drawers overflowing with fresh herbs and flowers. Cart culture pillar Grilled Cheese Grill's double decker bus dining room stands sentry at the entrance, a beacon for the steady stream of neighborhood patrons, most of whom head straight for Captured By Porches, which operates on a simple, failproof model—stick a half dozen taps into the side of a bus, fill Mason jars with beer, and distribute them to people marveling at their good fortune to be able to drink excellent beer from the side of a bus. Next door, hip, holy little silver Guero, protected from the spirits of mala comida by ornate silver crosses, spiky succulents and prayer candles, serves up supremely fresh, tasty tortas, while across the way, laid back Wolf & Bear's prepares unique Iraqi and Israeli-influenced Middle Eastern food like the sabich, a warm pita spread with hummus and mango pickle purée and stuffed with sliced boiled egg, cucumber, pickles, onions and fresh greens. And in Burrasca, the immaculate green lattice-trimmed cart hugging the southwest corner, Florentine transplant Paolo Calamai makes from-scratch inzimino, ribollita, wild boar pappardelle, and salsa verde-slathered pork loin paninos on homemade Tuscan-style rolls so authentic (read: saltless), you think you've been transported to Italy. You weren't really though, so, see you back here next Sunday, say around 2pm?

MUST EATS

Guero's Diablo bolo, Wolf & Bear's Olea, Burrasca's inzimino, Grilled Cheese Grill's Cheezus

SIDE DISH

If the weather is quarrelsome, you and your meal can take refuge inside the Grilled Cheese Grill's double decker bus.

DETAILS
- Covered seating available
- Street parking is free and generally easy to find

HOURS

Guero
TUE-SUN ... 11:30am-9pm

Wolf & Bear's
DAILY 11am-9pm

Burrasca
TUE-SAT ... 11:30am-7pm
SUN 11:30am-3pm

Grilled Cheese Grill
DAILY .... Hours vary

. . . .

113 SE 28TH AVENUE

eatwolfandbears.com • *burrascapdx.com*
facebook.com/gueropdx • *grilledcheesegrill.com*

. . . .

$$$$ *Some carts are cash only, ATM on premises*

PODNAH'S PIT BBQ

BARBECUE *in* **VERNON**

My family isn't exactly barbecue savvy, and childhood barbecues were scary business, marked by great roaring bursts of flames from lighter-fluid happy amateurs. It wasn't until college that I discovered barbecue could be so much more than black burgers and chicken breasts that tasted like shoe leather, thanks to my dorm mate Joe, who grew up on a Nipomo ranch and learned his AB'Cues while still in diapers. Under Joe's careful watch, critical eye, and slowly drawled instructions to anyone he trusted to man the grill while he refreshed his 7 & 7, his homemade oak-powered barbecue pit turned out tender tri-tips, juicy beer-basted chickens, slabs of sizzling bacon, and perfectly-seasoned pork ribs...oh, those ribs. Gnawing on one, marveling at how it was somehow crispy, juicy, chewy and tender all at the same time—I wasn't sure how I'd lived without them.

These feelings resurface whenever I visit Rodney Muirhead's Podnah's Pit BBQ, Portland's revered Texas-style BBQ joint, where down-home charm goes hand-in-hand with some of the city's finest smoked pork and lamb spareribs, brisket, pulled pork, chicken, and trout. Rodney's secret to success is simple, "he don't mess with Texas," firing up his BBQ daily at 5am and cooking everything slow 'n low over oak. Since great BBQ can only be enhanced by solid sidekicks, order the iceberg wedge drowned in chunky blue cheese dressing, pinto beans and potato salad, the Frito Chili Pie (served in the bag), and of course, pecan pie with a dollop of cold whoop.

MUST EATS

Iceberg wedge, pork ribs, brisket plate, brunch migas, whatever the daily special is—fried chicken, lamb ribs, prime rib, etc.

SIDE DISH

Podnah's peerless BBQ and wildly-popular country brunch can mean big lines to eat, but their neighboring cantina, La Taq, helps alleviate/eliminate waiting pains with smoked brisket tamales and master bartender Kevin Ludwig's excellent cocktails.

DETAILS

• Reservations accepted for parties of 6-10
• Street parking is free and easy to find

HOURS

MON-THU	11am-9pm
FRI	11am-10pm
SAT	9am-10pm
SUN	9am-9pm

. . . .

1625 NE KILLINGSWORTH STREET

503.281.3700 • *podnahspit.com*

. . . .

**$$**$$ *Credit Cards Accepted*

POK POK

THAI *in* RICHMOND

I was not always a chicken wing-appreciating girl. I once thought them coarse; fuel for famished frat boys and beer-bellied sports fanatics, consumed by the heap at dens of digestive iniquity. But I was wrong, so wrong.

Because Pok Pok's intoxicating Ike's Vietnamese Fish Sauce chicken wings are like no other—fried to a perfect caramelized crisp and covered in a sticky sweet and spicy glaze sure to leave you licking, if not devouring, your own fingers just to get the last bit of sauce. Pok Pok turned me on to the wonder of the chicken wing just like chef/owner Andy Ricker has revolutionized long-held perceptions of Thai food with exotic and intensely flavorful dishes you'd be hard pressed to find outside of Thailand—not surprising, considering Ricker jets off to Southeast Asia several times a year on exploratory food prowls, returning with yet more startlingly delicious recipes that keep even the most frequent of Pok Pok diners on their toes and coming back for more—like a grilled boar collar rubbed with garlic and coriander root, spicy chopped duck salad with duck liver and lemongrass, turmeric-marinated catfish, and smoky grilled eggplant salad with boiled egg, pork, prawns, dry shrimp and plenty of crispy fried garlic.

All these exotic eats can create quite a thirst, so Pok Pok's capable bartenders are at the ready to mix you a refreshing sweet-tart drinking vinegar, Tamarind Whiskey Sour or Salted Plum Vodka Collins, and for the ultimate cool down, finish your meal with a Whiskey Soda Float—homemade bourbon ice cream swimming in cola and topped with Amarena cherries.

MUST EATS

Ike's Spicy Wings, roasted game hen salad, grilled boar collar, clay pot gulf prawns, whiskey soda float

SIDE DISH

Portland can't seem to get enough of what Andy Ricker's cooking, and Pok Pok outposts continue to spring up all over the city. Next to the mothership is the Pok Pok shack, for takeout and informal (covered) outdoor dining; across the street lies the Whiskey Soda Lounge—a quirky-cool annex with cocktails, beer slushies and drinking snacks; up the street is casual, crowded Sen Yai noodle house; and when in Northeast Portland, Pok Pok Noi is the spot to quench your wing craving.

DETAILS	HOURS
• Reservations accepted for parties of 5+ via the website	DAILY...... 11:30am-10pm
• Street parking is free and generally easy to find	

· ·

3226 SE DIVISION STREET
503.232.1387 · *pokpokpdx.com*

· ·

**$$$**$ *Credit Cards Accepted*

POR QUÉ NO

MEXICAN in BOISE/RICHMOND

A couple of years ago I visited a dear old friend who lives in the laid-back little fishing and windsurfing village of La Ventana, Mexico. My dear old friend is a bit of a trouble magnet, you might say, and over the course of the week I spent there, I was nearly arrested by the federales, wooed by a misogynistic Mexican poet, stung by a jellyfish, held up by a sinister cabbie, and on the last night, my ATV plunged off a cliff. But as I lay on the table at the La Ventana medical clinic getting a massive shot of painkiller in my heinie and reflecting on my adventure-packed visit, all the near death experiences faded away and all I could remember were…the tacos.

Soft, warm handmade tortillas piled with smoky, spicy grilled meats, fish, and shrimp, just-made salsa, a sprinkling of freshly-diced onion and cilantro, and a tart squirt of lime, washed down with an icy bottle of Pacifico or Mexican Coke…well, I'd like to think it was the memory of those tacos that pulled me back from the brink of death. That's how powerful the magic of a good taco can be. And when I need a taco fix with some feel-good Mexican atmosphere here in Portland, I head to Por Qué No.

The festive terracotta and aqua blue facades and vividly-colored kitsch blanketing the walls, the busy kitchen and buzzing dining room filled with mouthwatering smells and lively conversation, the cold Mexican beers, margaritas, and big jars of aguas frescas and horchata, and the spirited staff—it all takes me back to those happy moments spent in little Mexican taco shacks, in between losing five of my nine lives. Viva la Por Qué No!

MUST EATS

Housemade chips and guacamole, ceviche with spicy cucumbers, verduras tacos, chorizo tacos, Bryan's Bowl with shrimp

SIDE DISH

Both Por Qué No locations have creatively-crafted outdoor patios that are an excellent place to pass a summer afternoon with a bucket of beers (and tacos)...and thanks to powerful heating systems, they're winter, fall and spring-friendly too.

DETAILS

+ No reservations
+ Street parking is free and generally easy to find at both locations

HOURS

SUN-THU... 11am-9:30pm
FRI-SAT 11am-10pm

Happy Hour
WED-MON......... 3-6pm
TUE............. 3-9:30pm

· ·

3524 N MISSISSIPPI AVE. · 503.467.4149
4635 SE HAWTHORNE BLVD. · 503.954.3138
porquenotacos.com

· ·

$$$$ *Credit Cards Accepted*

PORTLAND FARMERS' MARKET

OPEN AIR MARKET *in* DOWNTOWN

The rest of the nation may mock Portland's Extreme Green attitude, dismaying unemployment rates, and hipster infestation, but frankly I think they're just jealous. After all, who else can boast nearly 50 farmers' markets within a 20-mile radius? And the granddaddy of them all is the Saturday Portland Farmers' Market, located on Portland State University's beautiful downtown campus.

There are certain things I've come to expect when visiting this vibrant market: **(1)** Each and every visit, as I approach the market after a slow walk through the stately South Park Blocks, I will be bowled over yet again by the sheer beauty and bounty spilling forth from the nearly 150 vendor booths. Every single time. **(2)** Me and my cup of Nossa Familia coffee will need to walk the market's Byzantine aisles, nooks and crannies at least twice to suss out the freshest produce, flakiest pastries, and finest lamb, beef, buffalo, salmon, and oysters, sampling Unger Farms' berries, Unbound Pickling's green beans, and Chop charcuterie as we go. **(3)** I'll buy way more fresh kale, kohlrabi, rhubarb, artichokes, squash, blueberries, peaches, heirloom carrots, tomatoes, figs, and/or chanterelles than the shopping bag I brought can hold, so thank goodness for the market's Veggie Valet services. **(4)** I will order market vegetable-smothered huevos rancheros from Verde Cocina and a lamb pita from Tastebud and a slice of homemade peach raspberry pie from Lauretta Jean's and then I will *still* foolishly push my stomach over the edge with a strawberry shortcake from Pine State Biscuits, because I just can't help myself. And last but not least

(5) I will conclude my shopping session by reclining on the lawn and tapping/napping to the merry musical stylings of a local bluegrass band. For the full effect, I suggest you do the same.

MUST EATS

Ancient Heritage Dairy's Adelle cheese, Baird Family Orchards' Suncrest peaches, DeNoble's artichokes, Freddy Guys' hazelnuts, Fressen's beer bread, Gathering Together's Charentais melon, Jacobs Creamery's Bloomy, Prairie Creek Farm's potatoes, The Smokery's lox, Springwater Farm's chanterelles, Tastebud's wood-fired pizza, Three Sisters' tortillas verdes, Winters Farms' Shuksan strawberries, Zoe's pickled beets

SIDE DISH

Neighborhood farmers' markets are held every day of the week in Portland...how lucky are we?! Check out a list of my favorites on page 206, or refer to the Farmers' Market section on *underthetablewithjen.com* for all market locations and hours.

DETAILS	HOURS
• Street parking is metered and can be hard to find; There is a pay garage at SW Broadway and SW Hall	MAR-OCT.... 8:30am-2pm NOV-DEC....... 9am-2pm

. . . .

SOUTH PARK BLOCKS
SW PARK & SW MONTGOMERY

503.241.0032 • *portlandfarmersmarket.org*

. . . .

Vendors accept cash or official market tokens, which can be purchased with your credit card at the market info booth.

RACIÓN

SPANISH *in* DOWNTOWN

Regardless of your thoughts on molecular gastronomy/modern cuisine, I think most of us would agree that we're all a little better off after a warm bath…so why should octopus, salmon and abalone mushrooms be any different? At least, that's the theory driving this stylish downtown tapas bar, where two hard-working sous vide machines burble nonstop on the back counter, happy to let whatever chef Anthony Cafiero tosses their way have a leisurely soak before being plated in a deft flurry of unusual ingredients, exotic greens, spices, blueberry absinthe gel and lavender powder. Or something like that.

Working in a space roughly the size of a hot tub (the ultimate sous vide machine, obviously), the energetic Cafiero—with the help of one induction burner, a French-top range, his trusty plancha grill, and a very capable staff, calmly prepares his artful raciones, aka "tapas grandes," for the appreciative audience of patrons lining the U-shaped kitchen bar. They sip cider, Txakoli, and Hemingway's Blood cocktails while watching their own personal dinner theater, a casual choreography of ingredient assembly that gives pressure-cooked protein an extreme makeover. Shards of confit duck, foie gras crumbles, curried cous cous and pale gold gooseberries lie atop blueberry absinthe gel, a soft egg rests in a bed of sweet corn, popcorn pudding and purslane under a blanket of corn silk, tender chunks of Spanish octopus share a smear of romesco with slightly crunchy cubes of celeriac topped with lovage leaves and a dusting of shaved Tasmanian chocolate, and for dessert, a small dome of frozen lemon cream sits in deep purple grape jelly, surrounded by frozen Venus grapes encased in a thin, icy simple syrup shell, speared with shards of dehydrated chocolate mousse, then sprinkled with lavender powder. Which would undoubtedly also be lovely later in the evening, sprinkled in a warm bath.

MUST EATS

Spanish octopus, confit duck, sous vide egg, abalone mushrooms, frozen lemon cream

SIDE DISH

Dinner can be approached a couple of different ways—pick and choose from the raciones menu, or commit to the tasting menu (with optional, and excellent, wine pairings). With 24 hours notice, the kitchen is happy to accommodate vegetarian and pescetarian tasting menu requests too.

DETAILS

- Reservations accepted via phone and website
- Street parking is metered and can be difficult to find

HOURS

TUE-SAT 5-10pm

Happy Hour

TUE-SAT 5-6pm

. . . .

1205 SW WASHINGTON STREET

971.276.8008 • *racionpdx.com*

. . . .

$$$$ *Credit Cards Accepted*

ROE/BLOCK + TACKLE
SEAFOOD *in* RICHMOND

When chef Trent Pierce's beloved Hawthorne fish house Fin closed on Valentine's Day 2011 with little notice, it was akin to when the Red Sea parted...everyone was stunned, and they sort of froze, gaping disbelievingly, while the fish flopped around feeling forsaken, and then someone (not Moses this time, someone else) said something to the effect of 'we can make it through this together, there's something great on the other side,' and finally everyone moved forward and life went on, but with slightly less fish. (Yes, it's true that I slept through most of Sunday school, but I picked up the important bits.)

And lo and behold, two-and-a-half years and one ramen joint detour later, Pierce realized his long-held dream of re-opening a fish-focused restaurant, and since two of something nice is better than one, he opened adjoining seafood spots, in the same Division Street building. Roe, secreted away in the dimly-lit, minimalist back room, is a much-lauded 30-seat shrine to fish and foam, where every dish doubles as fine art and the all-in chef's tasting menu for two with moderate alcohol consumption will set you back a month's worth of good Golden Whitefish caviar (assuming your consumption is currently at one 2-ounce jar per day). Block and Tackle, just beyond Roe's doorway, is comprised of a long, narrow dining room and bar adorned with a ship's wheel, a few dozen glass floats, and a lot of netting, and serves affordable, unfussy fare with flare, like oyster shooters with smoked tomato citrus cocktail sauce, peel and eat prawns with cardamom aioli, seafood "charcuterie," and smoked mackerel with red plums. So the next time you feel like celebrating a miraculous escape from the pharaoh's armies with a multi-course tasting menu, or just a dozen Fanny Bays on the half shell and a bottle of sparkling rosé (the best way to celebrate anything, really), chart your course thisaway.

MUST EATS

Seafood charcuterie, crab dip, smoked mackerel, halibut fish and chips, butterscotch pudding

SIDE DISH

If your nasty little caviar habit has led to chowder budget shortfalls, sail in for Block + Tackle's happy hour—oysters are a dollar off, and Rainier tall boys, just a dollar.

DETAILS	HOURS
• Reservations accepted via phone or *opentable.com*	*Roe* WED-SAT 5-10pm
• Street parking is free and can be difficult to find	*Block + Tackle* WED-SUN 4-10pm
	Happy Hour WED-SAT 4-6pm

. . . .

3113 SE DIVISION STREET

503.232.1566   •   *roepdx.com*

503.236.0205   •   *blockandtacklepdx.com*

. . . .

$$$$ - $$$$ *Credit Cards Accepted*

RUBY JEWEL

Every so often, I'm just going about my day in the usual fashion, investigating a new food cart or quality-control testing the cava selection at my favorite wine bar, when I'm brutally blindsided by a fierce ice cream craving (by sometimes, I mean pretty much daily, rain or shine). When this happens, I follow the scent of fresh waffle cones to a Ruby Jewel scoop shop, stat.

Like many successful local epicurean entrepreneurs, Ruby Jewel creator and former cook Lisa Herlinger got her start at the Portland Farmers' Market, selling her creamy, cookie-clasped goods to a grateful ice cream sandwich starved public out of a big white cooler at a little pink cart. These days, her creations can be found in the likes of Whole Foods, New Seasons Market, and a long lineup of respectable eateries, but they are most beautifully displayed in the cheery downtown and North Portland scoop shops she runs with her sister Becky Burnett.

Ruby Jewel specializes in heaping bowls of handmade, small-batch artisan ice creams both traditional (Oregon Strawberry, Espresso, Fresh Mint Flake) and less so (Chocolate Blue Cheese, Bacon Caramel, Salted Black Licorice), tempting "cow-free" vegan offerings like the Lemon Mint Ice, make-your-own ice cream sandwiches, and bliss-inducing sundaes like the coffee caramel sauce and candied espresso beans-topped The Buzz, all crafted with locally and responsibly-sourced ingredients and hormone-free dairy products. And forget about gummy bears and Oreo crumbles—Ruby Jewel's artisan toppings include housemade marshmallows, candied coconut, rosemary pecans, peanut brittle, and exotic sea salts from The Meadow, Ruby Jewel's NoPo neighbor and Portland's salt authority. There are also pre-packed pints and DIY ice cream sandwich kits, ideal in case a craving sneaks up on you outside of normal business hours. It happens, trust me. You may as well be prepared!

MUST EATS

Hazelnut with honey bar, chévre with spiced peach jam, peppermint hot fudge, Kiss My Mint sundae, ginger peach ice cream sandwich

SIDE DISH

If you've seen Ruby Jewel's darling pink-fringed umbrella cart around town and wished you could have one of your very own, well, you can't, but you *can* arrange to have them bring theirs to your birthday party, work BBQ, food festival, and/or front yard.

DETAILS

+ Street parking is free and easy to find at the NoPo shop; metered and can be hard to find downtown

HOURS

DAILY............12-10pm

. . . .

3713 N MISSISSIPPI AVENUE ✦ 503.505.9314
428 SW 12TH AVENUE ✦ 971.271.8895
rubyjewel.com

. . . .

$$$$ *Credit Cards Accepted*

SAINT CUPCAKE

BAKERY *in* DOWNTOWN/SUNNYSIDE

When I was a kindergarten teacher*, I had to replace Soggy, the class fish, at least once a month due to the overenthusiastic "Fish Feeder" dumping the entire container of food in the bowl, resulting in Soggy's fatal overindulgence. Everyone knows goldfish can't stop eating in the face of irresistible deliciousness. That pretty much sums up my relationship with Saint Cupcake, a magical land where it always smells like fresh-baked cookies, and where neat rows of cupcakes wink from behind their glass curtain; calling your name, their wrappers unfurling themselves in your fingers, their frosted caps somehow making their way between your lips, again and again and again…yes, it's like that.

Saint Cupcake owner and "Chief Baking Officer" Jami Curl's signature creations come in a prismatic palette of match-made-in-heaven flavors, from the traditional buttercream-topped vanilla, to carrot cake with cream cheese frosting, to the toffee-chip-studded Toasted Coconut Cream and rich, gooey vegan German chocolate. But the menu doesn't stop there—it woos with alder-smoked chocolate chip cookies, Saigon cinnamon rolls, syrupy sticky buns, dark chocolate-drizzled hazelnut brioche, Melty Goods sundaes and ice cream sandwiches, and most dangerous of all, the come-hither Who Needs a Brownie? cookie, which makes my knees go weak at first glance. The only reason I haven't been found belly-up in the swimming pool, dead as a doornail from a Saint Cupcake overdose, is because sweets cost money, and eventually one runs out of money and has to waddle home. If you share Soggy and I's propensity to succumb to edible overload and are afraid to go inside Saint Cupcake for fear of blacking out and waking up buried in cake crumbs, they do deliver, and they also offer a unique Saint Cupcake Singing Telegram service, because nothing says "I Love You" like a cupcake-bearing stranger serenading your sweetie with The Beatles' "And I Love Her" as the entire office looks on. *No really, I was! For four looong years. I retired early.*

MUST EATS

Toasted coconut cream cupcake, Who Needs a Brownie? cookie, pecan pie bar, bonbonbunbun, oatmeal chai cookiewich

SIDE DISH

Steadily expanding her sweet empire, Jami opened tiny tasty Quin Candy Shoppe in downtown's Union Way, with a wall of artisan chocolates and her own line of handcrafted candies.

DETAILS	HOURS
• Street parking is free and easy to find at the SE shop; metered and difficult to find at the downtown shop	*SW Location*
	MON-FRI 8:30am-6pm
	SAT 9am-6pm
	SE Location
	MON-SAT 10am-9pm
	SUN............ 10am-5pm

. . . .

1138 SW MORRISON STREET • 503.473.8760

3300 SE BELMONT STREET • 503.235.0078

saintcupcake.com

. . . .

$$$$ *Credit Cards Accepted*

SALT & STRAW

ICE CREAM *in* VERNON/RICHMOND/NORTHWEST

Some mornings, you're sitting in your kitchen, reading *Gastronomica* and seeing how many malt balls you can fit in each cheek, wondering if you really should have eaten those last six breakfast tacos and contemplating becoming a healthier person, maybe going on the Kumquat Diet or a radish juice fast, and then ping! A calendar alert reminds you that Salt & Straw opens in five minutes. And suddenly you're on your feet and out the door, leaving a trail of malt balls in your wake. Pushing the scoop shop door open a few moments later, you're instantly cocooned in a warm cloud of waffle-cone scented air, and a row of super scoopers beam at you from behind the counter, tiny silver tasting spoons in hand, asking what flavors you'd like to try. Sea Salt with Caramel Ribbons? Coffee and Bourbon? Arbequina Olive Oil? Anything! Everything! Whatever you want! It's yours! Your inner five-year-old self faints dead away, your love handles jiggle ecstatically, and you just wanna shoop scoop ba-doop, scoop ba-doop, scoop ba-doop ba-doop ba-doop.

The anything-and-everything tasting policy, coupled with their devotion to using high quality Oregon ingredients and close collaborations with the best local chefs, farms and artisans, are a few of the reasons the dynamic duo (and cousins) behind Salt & Straw, head ice cream maker Tyler Malek and culinary director Kim Malek, have enjoyed such enormous success since they first debuted their adventurous small-batch ice creams. So much so, that in just over two years, they've gone from the humble confines of their darling trademark striped awning topped push cart to a trio of handsome salvaged wood lined scooperias on Portland's most popular foodie thoroughfares. Which means that your Pear with Blue Cheese and Freckled Woodblock Chocolate comes with a price—making it through the long, snaking lines of fellow scoop, sundae, shake and float lovers. So, pack a few malt balls to snack on, prepare to make small talk, and start planning your tasting trajectory.

MUST EATS

Stawberry Honey Balsamic, Pear with Blue Cheese, Almond Brittle, Chocolate Gooey Brownie, Arbequina Olive Oil

SIDE DISH

If you've sampled and sampled some more and still can't decide, get the $9, four-mini-scoop tasting flight. Crisis averted.

DETAILS	HOURS
‣ NE and SE street parking is free and easy to find; NW street parking is free and can be difficult to find	*NE & SE Locations* DAILY . . . . 11am-11pm *NW Location* DAILY 7am-11pm

. . . .

2035 NE ALBERTA ST. ‣ 503.208.3867

3345 SE DIVISION ST. ‣ 503.208.2054

838 NW 23RD AVE. ‣ 971.271.8168

saltandstraw.com

. . . .

$$$$ *Credit Cards Accepted*

SAUVAGE

WINE BAR *in* BUCKMAN

It's dusk, and you're sitting by yourself at a polished, votive-lit bar in a sexy inner Southeast wine bar, sipping a very nice Viognier and checking out the lovely old brick walls looming over a long communal table full of laughing, chatting friends catching up over bottles of Roussanne and deviled quail eggs, and the rack of wine barrels next to bistro tables full of loved-up twosomes making kissyfaces over their Prosecco and oysters with Coho roe. You're *trying* to get a good view of the adjoining winery through the glass-paned doors, but are blocked by a giddy glassy-eyed couple whose conversation alternates between exclaiming how happy they are to have gotten a sitter for their new baby and how much they miss their new baby, when suddenly, you are nearly knocked flat off your stool by the blinding, dismaying insight that something very important and very *meaningful* is missing from your life. Something like a winery in your kitchen.

Sauvage owner/winemaker Jesse Skiles doesn't have these sorts of doubting moments, because he already has a winery in his kitchen. After establishing Fausse Piste urban winery, the Culinary Institute of America-trained chef then opened adjoining Sauvage enopub, the name a nod to Skiles' devotion to wild untamed yeasts and letting them do their thing. The one-page menu of decadent small plates, designed to complement sommelier Jeff Vejr's 50+ glass pour list of sustainable, natural, organic and biodynamic wines, is characterized as "modern farmhouse cuisine," in other words, dishes you might eat in a farmhouse if a Top Chef was cooking, dishes like chilled prawns with corn custard, elk carpaccio, bacon-wrapped octopus, and ricotta gnudi in pheasant ragu. You'll still be thinking about the whole experience as you lie alone in your twin bed later that night, absently gnawing the peaches-and-cream strudel you got to go, pondering whether maybe, just maybe, it's time you called that cute contractor from your I Need More Friends! Meetup group, and asked him...if he could rearrange a few walls and install a press, pump, and fermentation tank in your kitchen.

MUST EATS

Oysters with roe and granita, deviled quail eggs, albacore tartare, ricotta gnudi, strudel

SIDE DISH

There are a handful of Fausse Piste wines on the list, and if you try one and fall in love with it, you can buy a bottle to go, to drink alone at home or *perhaps* share with your cute contractor.

DETAILS	HOURS	
• Reservations accepted for parties of six or more	TUE-THU	5-10pm
	FRI-SAT	5-11pm
• Street parking is free and easy to find	*Happy Hour*	
	TUE-FRI	5-6pm

. . . .

537 SE ASH STREET
971.258.5829 • *sauvagepdx.com*

. . . .

**$$$**$ *Credit Cards Accepted*

SCREEN DOOR

SOUTHERN *in* KERNS

Surveying the weekend-morning line outside Screen Door, it's immediately apparent that you're going to need some reinforcements before you invade this fortress of fried oyster Benedict and Bananas Foster French toast. Hot coffee, warm clothing, reading material/conversation skills, and if you have the crushing misfortune to miss the cut for the first seating, some grief counseling and a granola bar might be in order.

Come Saturday and Sunday mornings, rain, sleet, snow or shine, 'round the corner and halfway down the block, in twos, fours, and mores, some with entire flocks of children in tow, eager early birds wait patiently (some, semi-patiently) for their dose of Portland's heartiest brunch. The Screen Door kitchen crew incorporates local and organic produce and meat into what they describe as a "survey of the south"—a blend of low-country cuisine, rustic one-pot Cajun cooking, and fancy Creole fare that spawns flavorsome brunch *and* dinner dishes like cornmeal-crusted fried green tomatoes, buttermilk-battered fried chicken with tasso gravy, and praline bacon waffles. (Yes, praline bacon.)

The dining room is lined with cushy booths and accented with homey touches, creating a cheerful down-home dining experience that comforts both soul and belly. A long communal table accommodates large groups and families, even old-woman-in-a-shoe-sized ones, and when the restaurant is full, it's so loud that even if your little one got up on the wrong side of the crib, their grumblings really won't make a dent. Service is fast and efficient and the staff is attractive and good-humored, so if you don't yet have any children to keep you company in the Screen Door line but would like to have some someday, you might want to chat up your cute, friendly server.

MUST EATS

Cornmeal-crusted fried green tomatoes, praline bacon waffle, fried oyster Benedict, fried chicken, banoffee pie

SIDE DISH

At first glance, Screen Door's menu might send a non-carnivore fleeing for the nearest kale smoothie, but fear not—they have a daily menu of sophisticated vegetable specials like roasted cremini mushroom tart and slow stewed yellow-eyed beans.

DETAILS	HOURS
• Reservations accepted for parties of six or more	TUE-SAT 5:30-10pm
	SUN-MON 5:30-9pm
• Street parking is free and can be difficult to find	*Brunch*
	SAT-SUN 9am-2:30pm

. . . .

2337 E BURNSIDE STREET
503.542.0880 • *screendoorrestaurant.com*

. . . .

**$$$**$ *Credit Cards Accepted*

SIMPATICA DINING HALL

NEW AMERICAN *in* BUCKMAN

I have mixed feelings about big family dinners. Sure, they can be memorable opportunities to share good food, catch up with family news and gush over the chubby pink new nephew, OR, they can be confining and threatening social occasions where your mother makes rude public comments about your weight, your uncle disparages your career choices, and your boyfriend's crotchety grandmother calls you by his ex's name the entire night. Thankfully, you're far more likely to experience the former at Simpatica Dining Hall, which hosts communal "family-style" weekend dinners that brilliantly showcase both Pacific Northwest cuisine and Portland's incredible bounty of seasonal produce. The always changing prix fixe menu reads like the sort of gourmet lineup I dream of rustling up with all the beautiful food I buy at Portland Farmers' Market on Saturday morning, if only I'd gone to culinary school instead of journalism school— Dungeness-crab stuffed sweet peppers followed by an heirloom tomato tart with roasted fennel and lardo, wood-grilled Oregon albacore tuna and Viridian Farms Pocha beans, and fresh peaches and mint spooned over warm almond cake.

Since eating an unforgettable meal with genial and interesting strangers is communal dining at its best and makes for fast friends and excellent wine-sharing opportunities, before too long, you'll know the names of your new family-for-a-night's children, pets and first high school flame, and they'll know your favorite gelato shop, bakery and antacid, and thanks to

Simpatica's policy of thoroughly explaining each course as it's served, everyone will know what a Pocha bean is.

MUST EATS

Whatever you're served! Simpatica's menu changes weekly, and you won't know what you'll be eating until the menu is posted online. Or, sign up to receive their weekly newsletter and the menu comes to you, along with an RSVP link. Dinners vary in price, but tend to be between $35-$45.

SIDE DISH

Simpatica serves one of my favorite Sunday brunches in the city, and every time I go I agonize over the fantastic and ridiculously reasonable selection of seasonal brunch dishes before ordering what I already knew I would—the bavette steak with eggs over easy, a mimosa, and the panna cotta.

DETAILS

- Dinner reservations accepted via phone or website; brunch reservations accepted for parties of four or more
- Street parking is free and easy to find

HOURS

Dinner

FRI 7:30pm

SAT 7pm

Brunch

SUN 9am-2pm

. . . .

828 SE ASH STREET

503.235.1600 • simpaticapdx.com

. . . .

**$$$**$ *Credit Cards Accepted*

SMALLWARES

ASIAN *in* BEAUMONT

Sometimes, the element of surprise is an unsettling thing—like when the doctor informs you that his initial head count was slightly off and you're actually having triplets, or when you mistake the anchovy paste for toothpaste, or when you think you're getting a Le Creuset goose pot for Christmas, but your (ex) boyfriend actually gets you a fruit bouquet. And conversely, sometimes the element of surprise is a wonderful thing, like when your boss decides you need an unlimited lunch expense account, or a whiskey and cake bar opens in your apartment building, or you think you're getting a fruit bouquet for Christmas but your (new) boyfriend gets you a Le Creuset goose pot, or anytime you order a dish at Smallwares.

Surprises abound on chef Johanna Ware's menu, as the Midwestern-born Momofuku and Public alum makes her unique mark on the Portland dining scene with exotic "inauthentic Asian" small plates punctuated by "spice and aggressive flavors;" dishes like carrot gnocchi in nori puree, pale pink spot prawns with cherries and yuzu kosho, chicken lollipops served on the bone, crispy fried kale with candied bacon and mint, an ultra silky, spicy pork-topped mapo dofu, gently steaming crab noodle soup, and oxtail curry lent a fiery kick from Scotch Bonnet peppers. The drink menu holds yet more pleasant surprises, especially for minimalists, the excellent cocktails are simply dubbed "The Vodka," "The Whisky," and "The Tequila," while wines, sakes, and beers are organized by flavor—i.e., earthy, funky, rich—verses white or red, but if this throws you for a loop, the server is happy to help decipher.

Unless you're a native northeaster, you'll have to make the trek to sleepy Beaumont to claim your table in the modern, voguish red and black dining room, but as you wrap things up with the kaffir lime panna cotta and a black cardamom, tamarind and honey-kissed The Rum, you'll be glad you spent the rickshaw fare.

MUST EATS

Spot prawns, mapo dofu, fried kale, oxtail curry, kaffir lime panna cotta

SIDE DISH

If you're on the midnight prowl for late night salty-spicy drinking food, look no further than Smallwares' adjoining Barwares, which serves cocktails and snacks like candied peanuts, somen noodles, and pork skin ragu nightly until 1am.

DETAILS	HOURS
• Reservations accepted via phone or *opentable.com*	DAILY............5-10pm
	Barwares
• Street parking is free and generally easy to find	DAILY...........5pm-1am

. . . .

4605 NE FREMONT STREET

971.229.0995 • *smallwarespdx.com*

. . . .

**$$$**$ *Credit Cards Accepted*

ST. JACK

FRENCH *in* HOSFORD-ABERNETHY/NORTHWEST

If two heads are better than one, then two restaurants must be better than one, and if the two restaurants are attached and one of them is actually a bakery, *that* must be better than a private Living Room Theater showing of *Amélie*, a bottle of Cristal Rosé, and a bucket of bacon fat croutons.

Enter St. Jack, Portland's very own bistro-bakery dream team, an intimate two-headed Clinton Street corner eatery with a big welcoming front door painted the color of a tarte au citron, a convivial mirror-backed zinc bar, perfect lighting, and cozy bistro tables adorned with fresh tulips. At the north end, a double doorway joins St. Jack restaurant with St. Jack patisserie, which opens at 8am to supply this sleepy Southeast Portland neighborhood with Stumptown coffee, Smith Teamaker tea, and pastry chef Alissa Rozos' freshly-baked croissants, dark-chocolate glazed eclairs, feather light baked-to-order madeleines, savory goat cheese tarts topped with a baked egg, strawberry brioche, sablés au chocolat and savory tartines.

The restaurant menu reflects chef Aaron Barnett's affection for rustic French cuisine and the cafés of Lyon, spotlighting specialties like Cervelle de Canut—a quenelle of goat cheese and fromage blanc blended with shallots and garlic, tureens of puff pastry capped escargot, the lardon-loaded salade Lyonnaise, gnocchi with crayfish and fresh corn, terrifically tender lamb shoulder confit, and a hapless roast squab who arrives with its feet and head sticking out either end of a petite pot. If you find it hard to choose, just remember—two dinner entrées are always better than one, and three desserts are *always* better than two.

MUST EATS

Oregon albacore salade niçoise, braised escargot, lamb shoulder confit, smoked salmon tartine, madeleines

SIDE DISH

The St. Jack team decided it was high time they let Northwest Portland eat cake too, and thusly, you'll be able to get their famous made-to-order madeleines at their second location, in the Alphabet District (*1610 NW 23rd Ave., opening Jan. 2014*).

<table>
<tr><td>DETAILS</td><td>HOURS</td></tr>
</table>

DETAILS

- Reservations accepted via phone and *opentable.com*
- Street parking is free and generally easy to find

HOURS

SUN-THU....... 5-9:30pm
FRI-SAT 5-10:30pm

Happy Hour
DAILY............. 4-5pm

Patisserie
DAILY.......... 8am-3pm

· ·

2039 SE CLINTON STREET
503.360.1281 · *stjackpdx.com*

· ·

$$$$ *Credit Cards Accepted*

THE SUGAR CUBE

BAKERY *in* CONCORDIA

I'm inclined to believe that, like Wolverine, Squirrel Girl, and Michel Lotito, pastry chef extraordinaire Kir Jensen was born with inexplicable abilities—which I have dubbed Sugarpowers. How else can you explain her fantastical, always-evolving line of near-magical sweets like fleur de sel brownies oozing with bittersweet chocolate ganache and dripping grassy green olive oil, passion fruit panna cotta topped with fresh local blackberries, chocolate caramel potato chip cupcakes, citrus rosemary tea cakes buried in dollops of lemon curd, chocolate raspberry bread pudding, espresso pecan sandwich cookies, and whipped cream topped slices of warm bourbon brown butter honey pie?

Besides the five-star desserts, Kir serves light breakfast fare from her cozy, butter-colored bakery on the quiet end of Alberta Street, so you can start your day off right, with toast. Predictably, this is no ordinary toast, it's slices of Little T American Baker's Sally Lunn loaf spread with mascarpone and Bee Local honey, or homemade Nutella and a drizzle of olive oil, or almond butter, cinnamony caramelized bananas and a pinch of sea salt. It's *super*toast. Even if you promised yourself you'd just pop in for a cup of Ristretto Roasters coffee, there's no better time than the present to break silly promises, especially when maple olive oil granola and spiced buttermilk cornbread with molasses butter are at stake. Because when us mortals are up against sugarpowers like these, even if it's 8:15am, it's impossible to resist Kir's command: "*Always* save room for dessert."

MUST EATS

Olive oil brownie, chocolate-dipped Lord Bergamot shortbread, citrus almond teacake with lemon curd, plum crostata, bourbon brown butter honey pie

SIDE DISH

Home cooks can attempt to create their own renditions of Kir's incredible desserts, by picking up a copy of her cookbook, *"Sugar Cube: 50 Deliciously Twisted Treats from the Sweetest Little Food Cart on the Planet"* at your neighborhood Powell's bookshop. May the Sugarforce be with you.

DETAILS

- No reservations
- Street parking is free and easy to find

HOURS

WED-SUN 8am-5pm

....

3039 NE ALBERTA STREET

971.202.7135 • *thesugarcubepdx.com*

....

$$$$ *Credit Cards Accepted*

SWEEDEEDEE

NEW AMERICAN *in* HUMBOLDT

Every 10 years or so I turn on *Wheel Of Fortune*, mostly just to see if Vanna White has aged at all, but of course she hasn't, not even a day, and while I'm googling eternal youth potions, I keep one eye on the show, anxiously waiting for someone to get the word Sweedeedee, buy the letter 'e', get very excited when the board lights up like a Christmas tree, and then, because they haven't a clue what a Sweedeedee is, have to spin again and lose their turn. It's nerve-wracking.

If only they'd been a Michael Hurley fan, or even better, a patron of Eloise Augustyn and Annastacia Weiss's Sweedeedee, easily one of Portland's best breakfast spots, even if you have to wait a honey pie's worth of time to get your corncakes with bacon and braised greens. Here's how it works—first, you must wake up (very important), then make your way to Sweedeedee, order at the counter, claim a table (it's first-come-first-served), drink a restorative cup of neighborhood roaster Extracto's coffee, and devour the baked goods you bought from the small pastry case by the register when you put in your order—one blackberry cornmeal muffin, one slab of zucchini cake, one pecan roll, two chocolate chip cookies, and one whole honey pie. I mean, a slice is nice and probably all you really need, but once you taste Sweedeedee's transcendent rendition (Augustyn is a former Random Order Bakery manager, which helps explain the pie proficiency), you're going to want the other seven slices you left behind, so save yourself the trip back through the line.

And almost invariably, the moment you've finished the last rich, golden bite of honey pie, your breakfast arrives. Say a blessing to the gods of Oregon bounty, then dig into your bowl of roasted potatoes, smoked trout and salsa verde, or your egg and homemade brioche laden breakfast plate, or your second honey pie. Afterwards, walking back to your compact SUV, bike, or bus stop (there's one right in front), you'll be thinking that the word _th_r_al doesn't even begin to do your meal justice.

MUST EATS

Berry cornmeal muffins, house granola with seasonal fruit, Baker's Breakfast, smoked trout plate, a honey pie

SIDE DISH

If you'd like to place a standing order of one Sweedeedee honey pie a day, and I hope you do (and I also hope you're my neighbor), just call them; special pastry orders are welcome and generally require a day's notice.

DETAILS
+ No reservations
+ Street parking is free and easy to find

HOURS
MON-SAT....... 8am-4pm
SUN............. 8am-2pm

5202 N ALBINA AVENUE
503.946.8087 • *sweedeedeepdx.tumblr.com*

$$$$ *Credit Cards Accepted*

TABOR BREAD

BAKERY *in* MT. TABOR

The first time I sat down at the bar facing this cozy Mt. Tabor bakery's huge wood-fired brick oven, ready for my front row view of an artisan loaf's journey from yeast to feast, I heard a strange, disembodied voice. *"The peel,"* it moaned. *"Watch the peel."* I was a bit freaked out, after all, I just wanted to relax and watch some boule bake, the last thing I needed was a nosy bakery ghost ruining my bread buzz. I turned slightly, to see a kindly staff member smiling at me. "Watch out for the peel," she said, pointing to a long-handled wooden paddle suspended in midair, just as a baker reached up, plucked it from its perch, reared back and stabbed it deftly into the oven's innards. "Don't want it to hit you in the nose." Since I didn't really have time that week for a nose job, I switched seats and watched the action from afar, shielding my face with a gingerbread cake just to be safe, until my neatly-wrapped herbed egg salad sandwich arrived and I had to dash back to the office. It was high adventure, to be sure.

The first retail bakery in Portland to mill its own flour and bake all its bread in a wood-fired oven, this charming neighborhood spot is raising the bread bar, with head baker Cory Mast producing rich, dense, and intensely flavorful Red Fife boules, polenta batards, Kamut flour baguettes, and rye Pullman loaves with sunflower and pumpkin seeds, all made with local Camas

Country Mill grains ground fresh daily on a constantly-whirring Austrian mill you can watch through the window. But since man and woman cannot allegedly live on bread alone (even house-milled, wood-fired whole grain bread), the pastry case is stocked with pastry chef Jocelyn Barda's superb work—spelt flour sticky buns, strawberry rhubarb galettes, blueberry coffeecake, streusel-topped cranberry oat muffins and currant orange caraway scones, all of which are both divinely delicious *and* can help safeguard your nose should the peel ever get into the hard cider and go on a rampage.

MUST EATS

Buckwheat chocolate chip cookie, cinnamon swirl bread, toast and jam, shortbread, cucumber and goat fromage blanc sandwich

SIDE DISH

Tabor Bread owner Tissa Stein, a longtime tango enthusiast, occasionally clears the floor and holds a traditional tango gathering known as a milonga, turning the entire place into a scene from *True Lies*. Call or ask at the register for more info.

DETAILS	HOURS
• Street parking is free and easy to find	WED-FRI 7am-6pm
	SAT-SUN 8am-4pm

5051 SE HAWTHORNE BOULEVARD

971.279.5530 • *taborbread.com*

**$$**$$ *Credit Cards Accepted*

TANUKI

JAPANESE/KOREAN *in* MONTAVILLA

You can't help but love a restaurant that not only turns out some of the finest Asian food in town, but has also adopted as its namesake a tipsy, mischievous raccoon-dog with shapeshifting powers and oversized testicles. Scrappy Tanuki (the bar, not the legendary creature of Japanese folklore) models itself after a traditional izakaya—boozy bastions of well-earned post-workday beverages and bites served with a side of camaraderie, and as is such, chef Janis Martin's Japanese and Korean-influenced menu is punctuated by unusual and unusually-tasty drinking snacks like the spicy squid jerky and toasted pressed filefish, "stuff on sticks" (spiced duck heart skewers, anyone?), a hauntingly creamy, melt-in-your-mouth hamachi sashimi, and boldly-flavorful small plates like cinnamon tea quail eggs, octopus salad with mulberry ginger dressing, seared black cod and blood sausage, pork belly curry, and the "acquired taste, no-returns"-allowed natto.

The atmosphere can also be an acquired taste for more traditional diners; Martin is a strong personality, and so is her restaurant. Japanese horror movies play on the television over the bar, pinball machines flash provocatively in a back corner, pungent scents permeate the loud, diminutive dining room, and the light is low enough that trying to Instagram your meal is pretty much futile, so you may as well just sit back and enjoy it instead. While you'll be happy picking and choosing from the always intriguing menu, the best way to eat here is omakase—

tell the server how much you want to spend, then relax, watch *Big Tits Zombie*, and await an unforgettable meal. Ringing with the clink of sake cups, the soft tap of chopsticks against bowls of spicy tantan noodles, and the buzz of animated conversation, Tanuki embodies the spirit of izakaya, big balls and all.

MUST EATS

Hamachi sashimi, bay scallop skewers, kimchi fried rice, black cod with blood sausage, tantan noodles

SIDE DISH

In accord with Martin's original vision of Tanuki being a sake retailer first, bar second, Tuesday and Wednesday nights will be devoted to sake tasting and selling, with a few snacks available.

DETAILS

+ No sushi, no reservations, no kids, no split checks, no parties over four (no room)
+ Street parking is free and can be difficult to find

HOURS

THU-SAT 5-10pm

Happy Hour

THU-SAT 5-6:30pm

8029 SE STARK STREET

tanukipdx.com

**$$**$$ *Credit Cards Accepted*

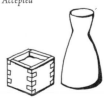

TASTY N SONS

NEW AMERICAN *in* BOISE

Jay-Z touts the Empire State of Mind, Steinbeck opined that Texas is a state of mind, and here in Portland, well, Brunch could probably be declared the official state of mind. As is such, brunch lines can reach epic proportions on Saturday and Sunday mornings, sometimes costing you upwards of an hour of your precious weekend. As the Grail Knight warned in *Indiana Jones and the Last Crusade*, "Choose your brunch line wisely." Or something like that.

Tasty n Sons is worth the wait. When you make your way to the front of the line (I recommend sitting at the bar, so you can watch the finely-tuned kitchen crew in action), order a Sriracha-laced Tasty Mary and a slew of dishes to share; they're offered in two portion sizes—smaller and bigger. Standouts include Auntie Paula's French toast—thick slices of Fleur de Lis Bakery's levain are dredged in ice cream batter before hitting the frying pan, the house frittata—stuffed with seasonal local produce like fava beans, green beans and caramelized onions and delivered to the table in a cast iron skillet, and anything involving biscuits—Tasty n Sons' biscuits are as light as a feather and as flaky as the last guy you dated.

Brunch beverages are in ample supply, and the Bloody Marys list includes a tequila-based Mayan Maiden, aquavit-based Belladonna, and the Tasty Jerk, which comes with a side of housemade beef jerky. If you had a rock star sort of night and can't be bothered to rise before 6pm, Tasty n Sons serves dinner too, with a few select items from the brunch menu joining hearty supper favorites like chicken and dumplings, lamb souvlaki, grilled quail with couscous and merguez, and the famous Toro Burger—a bacon, Manchego and romesco-topped meaty wonder borrowed from Tasty's sister restaurant, Toro Bravo. For a sweet brunchy finish, come full circle with a banana and caramel drenched Auntie Paula's French toast sundae.

MUST EATS

Auntie Paula's French toast, fried egg and cheddar biscuit with smoked guanciale, cumin maple glazed yams, steak and eggs with cornmeal pancake, warm chocolate chip cookies

SIDE DISH

Tasty n Sons has a downtown brother, Tasty n Alder, and with their similar aesthetics and menus, they're like fraternal twins who hang with different crowds. If downtown's hustle and flow has you famished, slip into Tasty n Alder's hearty midday happy hour (2-5:30pm)—the ribeye and $1 biscuits will fortify you.

DETAILS	HOURS
• Reservations accepted for parties of six or more	SUN-THU 9am-10pm
	FRI-SAT 9am-11pm
• Street parking is free and generally easy to find	*Happy Hour*
	DAILY 2:30-5pm

. . . .

3808 N WILLIAMS AVENUE

503.621.1400 • *tastyntasty.com*

. . . .

**$$**$$ *Credit Cards Accepted*

TEOTE

LATIN AMERICAN *in* HOSFORD-ABERNETHY

Remember your favorite childhood summer camp, the one where all the buildings were built from mismatched scrapwood and painted every color in the Crayola paint set, and there were images of the Virgin Mary everywhere, and each night after a satisfying meal of pork belly arepas and blackberry sage agua frescas, you'd sit on a curved cobalt blue tile bench around the huge firepit and sing campfire songs about plantains while drinking mezcal from the mess hall's Jaguar Bar? Well then, Teote is going to be a much welcome blast from the past, because it's got all of the above, without so much as a tendril of poison ivy or even one Khaki Scout, talking can of vegetables, or snotty twin sibling you never knew you had.

A beautifully-crafted brick and mortar incarnation of the beloved Fuego de Lotus food cart, chef/owner Michael Kennett's areparia does indeed feel like the adult summer camp of your dreams, complete with a bar on every level—the downstairs bar is just to the right of the Plantain Ripeness Meter, the picnic table-lined patio has one behind the swimming hole-sized fire pit, and upstairs, a few feet past the ornate "Carmadonna" tapestry hanging above the stairwell, sits the gorgeous mezcal-lined Jaguar Bar. Foodwise, the gluten-free menu revolves around the arepa, a Venezuelan staple that's essentially a warm, chewy corncake split in half and piled with savory fillings like pork belly in red chili maple sauce, chicken and avocado salad, and black beans with shredded cabbage and salsa verde. If corncakes aren't your camp food of choice, there are lamb chop and grilled short ribs plates, rice bowls, and of course, fried plantains. And over on the ever-evolving Bebidas board, you'll find seasonal agua frescas (with or without booze), housemade horchata spiked with Morita chili-infused vodka, and Michelada—draft Tecate dolled up with jalapeño serrano sauce, Worcestershire and lime juice. You know, just like you used to drink at camp.

MUST EATS

Fried plantains, El Diablo, Smokey Pollo, Frijol Negro, cacao and cinnamon arepa (served during weekend brunch)

SIDE DISH

At night, Teote's upstairs Jaguar Bar comes alive, serving a variety of mezcals by the half ounce and ounce, plus mezcal with chocolate flights, and mezcal with chocolate *and* coffee flights, or just the housemade chocolates by themselves.

DETAILS	HOURS
• No reservations	TUE-SUN 11am-11pm
• Street parking is free and easy to find	SAT-SUN 10am-2pm
	Happy Hour
	TUE-SUN 3-6pm & 9-11pm

. . . .

1615 SE 12TH AVENUE

971.888.5281 • *teotepdx.com*

. . . .

**$$**$$ *Credit Cards Accepted*

TORO BRAVO

SPANISH *in* ELIOT

I have yet to fulfill that lifelong dream of running with the bulls in Pamplona due to a low fear threshold and frugal pocketbook, so I just go to spirited little Toro Bravo instead—it is as much zesty good fun as its "brave bull" moniker, and far less likely to gore you to death.

Since opening this comely Northeast Portland tapas hotspot in 2007, chef/owner John Gorham has earned the undying devotion of Portlanders with his inventive menu of Spanish-inspired small plates presented with a Pacific Northwest twist—like a rich ragu made with roasted eggplant and grass-fed lamb, Oregon black truffle omelet oozing with salty, tangy Mahón cheese, squid ink fideos with rabbit sausage, and house Paella Toro teeming with chicken, shrimp, mussels, and spicy housemade chorizo.

Cocktails fly between the brisk bar and animated dining room, exponentially raising the glee levels at the tablefuls of girls out on the town, lubricating first dates holed up in the narrow, romantically-lit nook, and easing timid newcomers into the communal dining style implemented in half of the dining room. And since tapas would be forlorn without good wine, Toro Bravo obliges with a succinct wine list bearing very reasonably-priced Spanish and Pacific Northwest sips, but if you'd prefer to bring that bottle of Tempranillo you schlepped overseas from La Rioja this summer, corkage is a reasonable $15.

Even with six years under its toreador sash, Toro Bravo's popularity never wanes—every night, swarms of Portlanders and foodies-from-afar alike pack this cozy neighborhood hangout tighter than the balconies full of safely elevated onlookers lining the streets of Pamplona, making for great people-watching and eavesdropping (if you're into that sort of thing).

MUST EATS

Sheep's cheese with rose petal harissa, fried anchovies, piperade with duck egg, radicchio salad with olive toast, squid ink pasta

SIDE DISH

The Toro Bravo menu is a many-splendored thing, and if trying to decide what to order is giving you oxtail croquette sized hives, sit back and let the kitchen choose—the Chef's Tasting Menu is a steal at $30 per person.

DETAILS

- Reservations accepted Sun-Thu, for seven or more
- Street parking is free and can be difficult to find

HOURS

SUN-THU.........5-10pm
FRI-SAT 5-11pm

. . . .

120 NE RUSSELL STREET

503.281.4464 • torobravopdx.com

. . . .

**$$$**$ *Credit Cards Accepted*

TWO TARTS BAKERY

BAKERY *in the* **ALPHABET DISTRICT**

I once read an article in *Monocle* magazine about the allure of tiny things and humanity's seemingly innate love of all things small and cute, like puppies and midget weddings. Perhaps this explains my obsession with Two Tarts, the Northwest Portland bakery devoted entirely to producing small, cute cookies.

Tucked into an upscale mini-mall just off chic NW 23rd Avenue, head baker/Queen of Tarts Elizabeth Beekley and crew bake Lilliputian cappucino creams, pecan tessies, almond rhubarb macarons, pistachio shortbread, passion fruit creams, dark chocolate chews, and pumpkin whoopie pies, in accord with the philosophy that "the simple satisfaction that comes from a jewel-sized treat is undeniably rich." I'd have to agree that much pleasure can be derived from a small treat, although I'm ashamed to admit that one Two Tarts cookie is never enough and once I ate an entire baker's dozen of the Peanut Butter Creams (silver dollar sized peanut butter oatmeal cookies stuck together with peanut butter cream and drizzled with dark chocolate) in one sitting. Please don't judge me.

Follow your nose into this charming cookie nook and experience the buttery, hazelnut-rolled richness of a ganache-filled Hazelnut Baci, a teeny tiny fleur de sel sprinkled chocolate chipper, or a bite-sized ice cream cookie sandwich made with honey sesame snaps and a scoop of Two Tarts' lemon zest ice cream, and I think you'll agree there's nothing more joyfully small, cute and scrumptious than Two Tarts' cookies, except maybe a mini-bulldog wedding.

MUST EATS

Cappucino cream, fleur de sel chocolate chip, passion fruit cream, Earl Grey brownie, and at least a dozen peanut butter creams. And another dozen for your mini bulldog (at least that's who I say the second dozen is for)

SIDE DISH

Having mastered the tiny cookie, Elizabeth took on a sweet new challenge–establishing Two Tarts' sister bakery, Palace Cakes, which specializes in gorgeous, elegant cupcakes and layer cakes.

DETAILS

· Small parking lot out front; street parking is free and can be difficult to find

HOURS

TUE-SAT ... 10:30am-6pm
SUN 12-5pm

2309 NW KEARNEY STREET

503.312.9522 · *tartnation.wordpress.com*

$$$$ *Credit Cards Accepted*

VIKING SOUL FOOD

NORWEGIAN FOOD CART *in* SUNNYSIDE

Striding through the Good Food Here cart pod, I spied with my hungry little eye a shiny silver vintage Streamline trailer sailing proudly, the lettering on her prow identifying her as Viking Soul Food. Since Viking soul food had thus far eluded me in this life, I crossed the asphalt fjord to investigate. "For the valkyrie within," the menu promised. Turning to *Wiki* for clarification, I learned that valkyrie is actually an ancient Norse term for "chooser of the slain;" a gang of powerful temptresses that decide who will die in a battle, then escort the fallen combatants to the big mead hall in the sky. In their spare time, they romance heroes and transmogrify into swans. Now you know.

Viking Soul Food's chef/owner, Megan Walhood, who is not a valkyrie (that I know of) but *was* formerly a sous chef at Nostrana, grew up eating her Norwegian father's cooking and wanted to share this unique meatball and pickled cabbage punctuated cuisine with Portland. So she and charming co-owner/partner Jeremy Daniels opened their now-famous Airstream cart, serving a menu based on the Norwegian dietary staple *lefse*, a thin potato flatbread resembling a translucent flour tortilla, which they fill with enticing combinations both savory (think Akevitt-cured salmon, dill crème fraîche, pickled shallot and watercress, or Dungeness crab, roasted parsnip, artichoke hearts and hazelnuts) and sweet (lemon curd and spiced pecans, and lingonberries with homemade cream cheese), then fold into what look like little Viking burritos. Eating these vibrantly-flavorful Norwegian bundles while overseeing the battlefield of Good Food Here carts contending for the affections of the lunch crowd, I swore I could feel downy swan feathers sprouting along my forearms.

MUST EATS

Smoked salmon and dill crème fraîche lefse, Norse meatballs and Gjetost sauce lefse, lemon curd and spiced pecans lefse, caramel custard and dark chocolate sauce lefse, fish cakes

SIDE DISH

I highly suggest you "like" Viking Soul Food on Facebook, because Megan and Jeremy are constantly coming up with seasonal specials so inspired they will actually cause you to spring up out of your chair and hightail it to the cart immediately upon reading them. At least, this has been my experience.

DETAILS

+ Street parking is free and easy to find
+ Covered seating is available

HOURS

SUN, TUE-THU .. 12-8pm
FRI-SAT 12-9pm

. . . .

4262 SE BELMONT STREET
503.704.5481 + *vikingsoulfood.com*

. . . .

$$$$ *Credit Cards Accepted*

WAFFLE WINDOW

WAFFLES *in* RICHMOND

Holes in the walls can be dangerous things. In Rome, they bite your hand off if you tell a lie. In the Sonoran desert, they conceal ill-tempered western diamondback rattlesnakes, and in Alaska they are occupied by ravenous wolverines. In New York, they can give you a nasty bellyache. But here in kinder, gentler Portland, our holes in the walls produce divinely dense, chewy, yeasty Liège waffles. Take that, Rome!

'Tis the rare hole in the wall that can conjure up pearl sugar-crusted Belgian waffles, which is why I feel ever so fortunate that we Portlanders can boast the beloved Waffle Window, a tiny hollow in the side of the eclectic Hawthorne district's venerable Bread and Ink Café. A few steps off the main drag, sheltered by a red-and-white striped awning and flanked by overflowing hanging flower baskets, the Waffle Window's amiable waffle men and maidens take your order through the open top half of a bright blue Dutch door, disappear with a sweet smile, then magically return bearing elaborate works of waffle art like the Bananarumba—a mound of sliced bananas sprinkled with granola crunch, covered in whipped cream, and drizzled with banana caramel sauce; the decadent Three B's—pepper bacon, Brie, fresh basil, and housemade peach jam; and seasonal favorites like the Falling Leaves—a dark chocolate dipped waffle piled high with freshly sliced pears and raspberries, and topped with a feathery dollop of whipped cream and chocolate sauce.

And so the Waffle Window makes the world a better place, slowly but surely bolstering the reputation of holes in the walls everywhere, one Hot Fudge Sundae waffle at a time.

MUST EATS

Spring Fling, Farm Fusion, Nutella and banana, hot fudge sundae waffle, waffle ice cream sandwich (*with* optional upgrade to chocolate-dipped waffles)

SIDE DISH

There is a line of sidewalk tables along the brick wall surrounding the Waffle Window, for you to sit at and devour your Triple Berry Sundae waffle and sip green tea mint lemonade while observing the quirky Hawthorne foot traffic. This works out very well in summer, but when the nine long months of winter sock in, you'll end up with a pretty soggy waffle. Thankfully, Bread and Ink Café has graciously provided an indoor eating area for you and your waffle. Or, visit Waffle Window's Alberta Street sister shop, which has a sizeable waterproof dining area.

DETAILS	HOURS	
• No reservations	SUN-THU.......	8am-6pm
• Street parking is free and can be difficult to find	FRI-SAT	8am-9pm

. . . .

3610 SE HAWTHORNE BOULEVARD
971.255.0501 • *wafflewindow.com*

. . . .

$$$$ *Credit Cards Accepted*

WILDWOOD

NEW AMERICAN *in the* ALPHABET DISTRICT

Although it's theorized that no mortal man is technically perfect, for reasons involving a treacherous snake and a Honeycrisp apple*, let's be honest here—we all have that one friend who is irksomely flawless. Parking spots appear from a mysterious mist when they pull up to a crowded restaurant. They never miss happy hour by three lousy minutes, but if they did, the smiling server would fawningly offer to override the POS system to give them an extension. They can accidentally eat 48 Sahagún Luscious Caramels in one sitting without gaining even one nano-ounce (okay, so they probably wouldn't accidentally eat 48 caramels in one sitting to begin with).

As restaurants go, Wildwood is that friend. Gracefully occupying the corner of NW 21st and Overton in Portland's elegant Alphabet District, Wildwood is one of the city's original bastions of local, sustainable cooking, and continues to set the standard with a determined dedication to organic, seasonal, farm-to-table fare. Chef Dustin Clark serves up classic Pacific Northwest-influenced dishes like heirloom tomato panzanella, Russet potato gnocchi with foie gras butter, and grilled confit of lamb in fennel-Fatalii pepper purée; and if you think that sounds pretty flawless, you should see the wine list. If you can't commit to the full dinner monty, try out happy hour in the bar—$5 will get you a glass of wine or one of five cocktails, and the well-rounded menu plies you with filling drinking snacks like potato croquettes with Green Goddess dressing, kimchi fried rice, and the mighty Wildwood burger, a juicy, housemade challah bun clad hunk of beef with crisp butter lettuce, Calabrian chili aioli and caramelized onion purée. Which, naturally, your flawless friend wouldn't drip so much as a drop of on their always-spotless white shirt.

While I can't actually prove the forbidden fruit was a Honeycrisp apple, it would make sense, because everyone knows Honeycrisps cannot be resisted.

MUST EATS

Grilled flank steak and arugula pesto linguine, aquavit-cured salmon bruschetta, brick oven roasted mussels, succotash-stuffed poblanos, Wildwood burger

SIDE DISH

At Wildwood, every Sunday is No Somm-Sunday—they give the sommelier the night off and let you sneak your favorite wines in without a corkage fee (limit two).

DETAILS	HOURS
• Reservations accepted via phone or *opentable.com*	MON-FRI 11:30am-10pm
	SAT-SUN 5:30-10pm
• There is a private parking lot, and street parking is free and easy to find	*Happy Hour*
	MON-FRI 4-6pm

. . . .

1221 NW 21ST AVENUE

503.248.9663 • *wildwoodrestaurant.com*

. . . .

$$$$ *Credit Cards Accepted*

WOODSMAN
TAVERN & MARKET

NEW AMERICAN *in* RICHMOND

One of the greatest, but somewhat tricky to pull off, culinary experiences is the safari supper, a.k.a progressive dinner. The idea being that you host a fun, food-loving group of friends for one course at your home, then caravan to the next host's abode, and 6-10 courses later, there's not just one, but 6-10 thoroughly disheveled kitchens and dining rooms all over the city. Er, I meant to say, the idea being that you create an unforgettable roving repast. If only there was a way to achieve that level of dining diversity without getting so much as a drop of borscht, squid ink aioli, blueberry balsamic reduction or ruby port on 6-10 beige sofas! Enter Division Street, where top restaurants and cocktail bars are opening so fast and thick, you'll hardly get half a blister walking a 6-10 restaurant route. It is, essentially, a low-risk progressive diner's dream.

How this dapper dinnerhouse plays into your safari supper route, you'll have to decide. After all, with Portland spirits sorcerer Evan Zimmerman crafting puckery Omaha Sours and 24-karat gold-accented Bentley cocktails at the always-lively bar, it would be a natural kickoff. But then again, when you skim the starters menu and catch wind of the burrata in warm Calabrian chili sauce and grand seafood platter (perfect for sharing), you might think of making it the appetizer stop. Of course, nobody's going to complain if you decide to assign it the entrée course, after all, the whole grilled trout in "crazy water" is a local legend. And were this the group's final pre-Victory Bar dessert destination (because obviously, Victory Bar is your nightcap stop), there might not be a more sweetly elegant last rite than the pistachio cake with cardamom ice cream and plums. Then, since you're only human, and safari supper routes can be slightly more spontaneous when someone isn't expecting you to come slosh ruby port all over their sofa at a prescribed time, you might as well have a Ship Of Fools cocktail for the road.

MUST EATS

Oysters, ham plate, drummettes, whole trout, fig jam tart

SIDE DISH

Next door to the Tavern, the European-style Woodsman Market sells fresh produce and eggs, cheese, charcuterie, wine and other genteel sundries, as well as homemade sandwiches and a chocolate pudding so exceptional, you'll want to buy it by the barrel (you can't though, sorry for getting your hopes up).

DETAILS	HOURS
• Reservations accepted via phone and *opentable.com*	DAILY.............5-10pm
	Brunch
• Street parking is free and generally easy to find	SUN............10am-2pm
	Market
	DAILY...........9am-7pm

. . . .

4537 SE DIVISION STREET

971.373.8264 • *woodsmantavern.com*

. . . .

**$$$**$ *Credit Cards Accepted*

XICO

MEXICAN *in* RICHMOND

Although I plan on being cryogenically frozen with my hairless Persian chinchilla and a bottle of Krug, I'll still want a commemorative plaque or perhaps just a small chocolate headstone in place when I go to the big Patisserie in the Sky, because I will need a spot for people to leave treats on Día de Los Muertos, the ancient and revered Mexican holiday where the living honor the not-living by placing their favorite foods on their graves. And since we're on the topic, I'm requesting a pile of Xico's sopaipillas as one of my afterlife snacks, because on my list of foods I think about when I get up and before I go to bed, Xico's otherworldy (hopefully!) lard puffs are pretty far up there.

Since chef Kelly Myers serves them several different ways, if you're in the mood, you can actually have three courses' worth—start with two fresh sopaipillas served alongside a casuela of velvety Sonoran refried beans, chorizo, Muenster cheese and red salsa, have them as a side with your slow-roasted goat barbacoa to help sop up the salsa borracha, and for dessert, request the "dulces con salsas" version, which means they come rolled in cinnamon and sugar with dulce de leche and chocolate-coconut sauce for dipping. Admittedly, you might have to release the top button of your chinos somewhere along the line, but no one will notice, thanks to the romantic lighting in this gorgeous dining room, a white-walled, marble bar lined space accented with bold splashes of color lent by fresh flower arrangements and festive fabrics and the bright, spicy salsas that are one of

Myers' greatest kitchen feats. Should you be tempted by the stellar mezcal menu, do try one of the flights, which arrive in tall crystal shot glasses with a side of worm salt. Then, when you're finished, order a glass of the Woodblock drinking chocolate with mole-spiced whipped cream and mezcal upgrade, plus one more sopaipilla for the road.

MUST EATS

Sopaipillas, vegetarian torta, albacore tacos, roasted whole trout pozole, flourless Woodblock chocolate cake

SIDE DISH

Xico serves a tasty seven-item "lunx" out of the kitchen's side window (just follow the signs), which you can either take to go, or eat in—dining room seating is available year-round, and in fair weather, the pretty back patio is open for al fresco business.

DETAILS	HOURS
• Reservations accepted via phone or *opentable.com*	WED-SAT ... 11:30am-2pm
	SUN-THU 5-10pm
• Street parking is free and gnerally easy to find	FRI-SAT 5-11pm
	Brunch
	SUN 10am-2pm
	Happy Hour
	MON-FRI 5-6:30pm

. . . .

3715 SE DIVISION STREET

503.548.6343 • *xicopdx.com*

. . . .

**$$$**$ *Credit Cards Accepted*

TOP 10 FOOD EVENTS

EAT MOBILE
April · *wweek.com/portland/eatmobile*

With Portland's food carts propagating like rabbits, it can be hard to get around to all of these wheeled gastro-wonders. So the *Willamette Week* brings the best of the cart world to you.

TASTE OF THE NATION
May · *strength.org/portland*

Yes, there's an uncomfortable irony in fighting hunger with unabashed gluttony. If you can get past that part, this is one of the year's best gatherings of local chefs, wineries, and food lovers.

PIX'S BASTILLE DAY BLOCK PARTY
July · *pixpatisserie.com*

A joyfully raucous celebration that begins with a five-kilometer "Mini Medoc Fun Run," ends with a twilight dance party, and sandwiches a Grape Stomp, Waiter Race, and champagne-sabering demo somewhere in the middle.

COUNTER CULTURE
July · *anneamie.com/counterculture*

This intimate pre-International Pinot Noir Celebration event pairs beloved local chefs with some of the weekend's best wines and breathtaking Oregon wine country views. And hammocks.

IPNC SALMON BAKE & PASSPORT TO PINOT
July · *ipnc.org*

Saturday's Salmon Bake stars alder-roasted wild salmon and fine wines, while Sunday's Passport to Pinot unites 30 international winemakers and wine-loving bites from noted local restaurants.

FESTA ITALIANA
August • *festa-italiana.org*

Hey mambo, eat like an Italiano at this spirited annual ode to the Boot that fills Pioneer Courthouse Square with freely-flowing wine, carbs, and music for three glorious summer days.

FEAST PORTLAND
September • *feastportland.com*

Pack your handbag/manbag with digestive enzymes, a backup button-down lest you lose control of your maple-glazed pork belly, and a Montblanc to capture celebrity chef autographs—you're headed to Portland's biggest, swankiest food festival.

POLISH FESTIVAL
September • *portlandpolonia.org/festival*

Your yearly excuse to eat way too many pierogi, kielbasa, gołabki, placki and paczki, drink too much Polish beer and honey wine, and dance the polka as if no one's watching.

GREEK FESTIVAL
October • *goholytrinity.org/cGreekFest.html*

The Holy Trinity Greek Orthodox Church's annual fundraiser has it all—spit-roasted lamb, live music, energetic folk dancing, and Greek wine bracing enough to peel the paint off your villa.

PORTLAND FERMENTATION FESTIVAL
October • *portlandfermentationfestival.com*

This funky festival unites experienced picklers and fermenters and introduces the uninitiated to a brave, stinky new world filled with kraut, kefir, tempeh, cider, kimchi, kombucha, curtido, miso, mead, and the ever-lovable natto.

FARMERS' MARKETS

'Round these parts, we take our farmers' markets very seriously. Part shopportunity, part feastival, beautiful, bountiful open-air farmers' markets sprout like wild mushrooms in every corner of the city, brightening the lives and larders of our fair citizens with farm fresh produce, artisan cheese and charcuterie, just-baked breads and pastries, local tipples and coffee, blooming bouquets, a smörgåsbord of prepared eats, and live music for dancing off the calories accrued snacking on all of the above. Here are a few of my favorite local markets…

MONDAY

Pioneer Square Market
Jun-Sep, 10am-2pm
portlandfarmersmarket.org

TUESDAY

Lloyd Farmers' Market
Year Round, 10am-2pm
lloydfarmersmkt.net

OHSU Farmers' Market
Jun-Oct, 11am-3pm
ohsu.edu/farmersmarket

WEDNESDAY

Moreland Farmers' Market
May-Oct, 3-7pm
morelandfarmersmarket.org

People's Farmers' Market
Year Round, 2-7pm
peoples.coop

WEDNESDAY *cont.*

Shemanski Park Market
May-Oct, 10am-2pm
portlandfarmersmarket.org

Oregon City Market
Jun-Sep, 3-7pm
orcityfarmersmarket.com

THURSDAY

Buckman Farmers' Market
May-Sep, 3-7pm
portlandfarmersmarket.org

Northwest Market
Jun-Sep, 3-7pm
portlandfarmersmarket.org

FRIDAY

Kenton Farmers' Market
May-Sep, 3-7pm
interstatefarmersmarket.com

SATURDAY

Beaverton Farmers' Market
May-Nov, 8am-1:30pm
beavertonfarmersmarket.com

Hillsboro Farmers' Market
May-Oct, 8am-1:30pm
hillsboromarkets.org

Hollywood Farmers' Market
May-Nov, 8am-1pm
hollywoodfarmersmarket.org

Lake Oswego Market
May-Oct, 8:30am-1:30pm
ci.oswego.or.us/parksrec

Portland State Market
Mar-Dec, 8:30am-2pm
portlandfarmersmarket.org

St. Johns Farmers' Market
Jun-Oct, 9am-2pm
sjfarmersmarket.com

SUNDAY

Hillsdale Farmers' Market
Year Round, 10am-2pm
hillsdalefarmersmarket.com

King Farmers' Market
May-Nov, 10am-2pm
portlandfarmersmarket.org

Lents International Market
Jun-Oct, 11am-4pm
lentsfarmersmarket.org

Milwaukie Farmers' Market
May-Oct, 9:30am-2pm
milwaukiefarmersmarket.com

Montavilla Farmers' Market
Jun-Oct, 10am-2pm
montavillamarket.org

Woodstock Farmers' Market
Jun-Oct, 10am-2pm
woodstockmarketpdx.com

For a full list of markets visit
underthetablewithjen.com

FACESTUFFER GUIDES

·

E-GUIDES
$.99 - $2.99 · *facestufferguides.com*

Since travel and food go together like Fred and Ginger, bread and Irish butter, and a trip to Paris and tomorrow, I've written a line of food-centric travel itineraries for fellow wandering foodlovers. Just download, pack your appetite, and go.

·

GUIDEBOOKS
$4.95 - $14.95 · *wordcake.com*

Stay tuned for upcoming Facestuffer Guides—my Portland drink guidebook publishes in spring 2014, and I'll also be releasing e-guidebooks to both the city's best herbivore-friendly offerings, and finest food carts.

·

FOOD TOURS
Times vary, prices start at $250 · *underthetablewithjen.com*

Yup, it's you and me, baby. I offer small-batch (groups of 2-6) private Facestuffer Food Tours, customized to your food fancies and whims, be they chocolate, hot chocolate, bourbon, pie, or hot chocolate bourbon pie.

10 BEST PLACES
TO LAY YOUR FACES

ACE HOTEL
1022 SW Stark Street
503.228.2277 • $95-$250
For the hip, vinyl devotees,
vagabonds-in-the-know
acehotel.com/portland

HERON HAUS
2545 NW Westover Road
503.274.1846 • $140-$215
For privacy seekers, well-
heeled couples, hill walkers
heronhaus.com

HOTEL DELUXE
729 SW 15th Avenue
503.219.2094 • $140-$280
For lovers, classic cinema
buffs, Greta Garbo
hoteldeluxeportland.com

HOTEL MODERA
515 SW Clay Street
503.484.1084 • $129-$209
For PSU parents, business
travelers, trendy couples
hotelmodera.com

HOTEL MONACO
506 SW Washington Street
503.222.0001 • $185-$430
For dog lovers, spa aficiona-
dos, the Mad Hatter
monaco-portland.com

INN AT NORTHRUP STATION
2025 NW Northrup Street
503.224.0543 • $129-$169
For families, Paley's Place addicts, streetcar enthusiasts
northrupstation.com

JUPITER HOTEL
800 E Burnside Street
503.230.9200 • $95-$350
For rock stars, aspiring rock
stars, the young and restless
jupiterhotel.com

KENNEDY SCHOOL
5736 NE 33rd Avenue
503.249.3983 • $115-$145
For families, history buffs,
well-adjusted retired teachers
mcmenamins.com

RIVERPLACE HOTEL
1510 SW Harbor Way
503.228.3233 • $165-$400
For yachtspeople, water signs,
and goose-watchers
riverplacehotel.com

THE NINES HOTEL
525 SW Morrison Street
877.229.9995 • $220-$450
For your wealthy aunt,
the fashion forward, Shaq
thenines.com

"TOP 10" INDEX

⬧

LATE NIGHT (10PM+)

⬧

REAL MEAL
HAPPY HOURS

⬧

🍴⊙

JEN'S FAVORITES

INDEX BY CUISINE

THANK YOU

This book was made possible by many helping mouths. A million thanks and green smoothie toasts to Mom, Dad, and Michael for being relentless and undaunted eaters; Michelle for her many years of eater-in-crime companionship; Jeff for his love, support, and spirits-fortifying Cacao runs; Marnie for always being a #superstar friend; Mona for the witty emails and general otherworldy glow; Sarah for her keen palate and enduring all those stinker dinners; and the lovely Portland Picnic Society girls for being all-around delicious.

And a billion shrimp on rye sandwiches and shots of Aalborg to the best editorial team ever—designer and friend extraordinaire Mette of the *Bureau of Betterment*, unflappable genius and White Knight of Dead Hard Drives Darin of *Refresh Media*, and the unstoppable, doesn't-miss-a-trick Shellie of *Type A Productions*.

ABOUT JEN

Jen lives in Portland with her imaginary mini bulldog and a *lot* of leftovers. Her hobbies include browsing grocery stores and farmers' markets, experimenting with recipes involving melted chocolate and lots of it, reading *The Onion*, taking pictures of pocket ninjas, trying new cavas, and thinking about lunch.

She has been a cook, food stylist, dessert caterer, and teacher, but these days, she writes about all the best things to eat and drink in Portland and beyond, for various media outlets and on her website, *underthetablewithjen.com*. She also runs *wordcake.com*.

LEFTOVERS

Portland chefs and restaurateurs can't stop opening restaurants, and I can't stop eating at them, so anytime you need the skinny on what's new and noshable, just check my website and social mediums. You can also subscribe to my weekly newsletter, *Table Scraps*—it's sassier than a cayenne-covered filbert, tastier than a Royale with cheese, funnier than a nitrous-oxide cupcake, livelier than a barrel of chocolate-covered espresso monkeys, and much better reading than the back of a cereal box or that Dear John letter you found propped up against the milk carton this morning.

•

For the latest Facestuffer news, tips, and updates, visit
WWW.UNDERTHETABLEWITHJEN.COM
Or follow @jenlikestoeat
on Twitter and Instagram.

• •

And please remember to eat well, and often.